the **right** light

First published in the United States of America by

Rockport Publishers, Inc.

33 Commercial Street

Gloucester, Massachusetts 01930-5089

Telephone: (978) 282-9590

Facsimile: (978) 283-2742

www.rockpub.com

ISBN 1-56496-616-x

10 9 8 7 6 5 4 3 2 1

Design: Leeann Leftwich

Photo Research: Debbie Needleman

Cover Image: Photographer: Ken Hayden/
The Interior Archive, Photodesigner: Jonathan Reed

the **right** light

LIGHTING ESSENTIALS FOR THE HOME   LISA SKOLNIK   NORA RICHTER GREER

CRAFT PROJECTS BY LIVIA MCREE

Dedication

To Caroline, Sasha, Anastasia and Theodora, who fill my life with light.

-Lisa Skolnik

Acknowledgments

This book would not be possible without the collaboration of Nora Greer, my co-author and project manager; Debbie Needleman, our photo researcher; and a great deal of help from many others.

First, my thanks to Martha Wetherill, acquisitions editor at Rockport, whose endless enthusiasm for design books is inspirational. Further thanks to the staff at Rockport who contributed to this effort, including Jay Donahue and Kristy Mulkern. Finally, in a visual book, superb graphic design is also critical; my thanks to Stephen Perfetto, who made this book as brilliant and dazzling as the subject matter.

I would also like to thank the many photographers, interior designers and architects whose work appears on these pages. Their efforts comprise the core of this book; without their creativity and vision this volume would not be possible.
-Lisa Skolnik

My gratitude to those who brought me closer to *The Right Light*, especially Lisa, Martha, and Jay. Thanks to Kristy for all her help. And, as always, to William.
-N.R.G.

Contents

Introduction

Lighting is one of the most routine features of our homes—so routine, in fact, that we usually take it for granted. Most of us live without second thoughts with the standard-issue, built-in lighting that comes with our abodes. Of course, we supplement the overhead lighting in each room with lamps and fixtures of every ilk, yet we often don't choose these sources of light for the right reasons. They may look good, or solve an immediate problem by providing the illumination that is needed for a specific task, but are they really the right light?

Just as we carefully weigh the style of furniture or the palette of colors we use in our homes, we must carefully weigh the way we light them. Lighting does far more than merely illuminate a room; it also sets the stage for every act that takes place in it. Besides emphasizing areas of importance or activity, or

__left
Uplights placed behind the bench reflect off the marble wall.

highlighting prized possessions, light can create the right ambience for a space, be it prosaic or dramatic. A beautiful room can fall flat if it is outfitted with inadequate lighting. The same is true of beautiful fixtures or lamps; they are worthless as light sources if unsuited to the tasks at hand.

The environment and ambience we establish in a space by lighting it a certain way also has a profound effect on many aspects of our psyche. Take efficiency and performance. We are more likely to be alert, energetic, and ready to work on a sunny day, which causes bright highlights and crisp shadows in a room. The opposite holds true on a drab day, when there is no contrast and that same room assumes a monotonous tone that lulls its occupants into lethargy. In essence, the difference between these two days is due to variations in the quality of natural light. Fortunately, artificial illumination can create contrasts in a room to simulate natural light, if necessary, and provide a stimulating environment.

Light does far more than provide the illumination we need for efficiency. It also affects our psychological well-being through the moods it creates; we feel calm and serene, industrious and alert, lively and enthusiastic, or romantic and relaxed. And it isn't just natural light that produces this effect. Making a significant impact with lighting is an intricate undertaking that calls for a careful balance of both natural and artificial light.

Yet lighting has long been underutilized as a home design tool for a number of reasons. For starters, it requires more planning than many other decorating tools. It is easier to settle for an overhead fixture and a few plug-in lamps than to implement more effective lighting treatments that require special wiring or structural changes. Also, lighting doesn't offer any obvious type of gratification; it is a subtle element that must be appreciated at the time of day or night when it is at work. Finally, lighting has not received the attention it deserves and requires simply because many homeowners are unaware of the impact it makes in a space and feel inadequate using it as a decorating tool. Instead of tackling the subject themselves—which can require some technical reading—or calling in a pro, homeowners ignore the challenge altogether.

While the generic options suggested above—simply adding ceiling fixtures and a smattering of lamps—have long been the default lighting solution in many rooms, these options are no longer a given. Savvy architects, designers, and do-it-yourselfers are finally considering lighting as a critical component of good home design. As well it should be; successfully balancing the functional and aesthetic aspects of lighting takes consideration, planning, and careful implementation on a room-by-room basis. Lighting should, and will, vary greatly between rooms, depending on its function in each and the homeowner's design goals. In this book, we discuss the basics of lighting— why we need it, how it should work in every part of a home, and how to set and achieve your design goals.

HANDCRAFTED LAMPS by Livia McRee
A creative way to decorate your home with personal, custom lighting is to make your own. The craft projects in this book will inspire you to do just that, and produce the perfect light for any place in your home.

Getting the Light Right

We take the meaning of the phrase "let there be light" for granted; illuminating a home in just the right way can be a far from heavenly task. In fact, lighting is such an important feature of our everyday lives that it should be considered when a room is being furnished or, ideally, still in the midst of design and construction. But few of us have the opportunity to build a space from the ground up or even to consider lighting before putting anything else in a room. So we play catch-up, installing lights where we think they should be or where we find we desperately need them.

Regardless of whether we are starting from scratch or backtracking to address inadequacies in the way a space is illuminated, it is critical to develop a lighting plan for each room that addresses both substance and style. The lighting should fulfill the utilitarian objectives of everyday life and at the same time complement a specific decorating style. In addition, a good lighting plan relies on a combination of natural and artificial lighting. It takes into account the available natural light, balancing it with the function, architectural components, and decorative features of a room or space.

left

In this bedroom designed by architect Nico Rensch, individual task lights placed at each side of the bed's headboard supplement the general overhead lighting. A translucent pull-up shade controls glare during the day and offers privacy at night.

START WITH NATURAL LIGHT Thanks to contemporary zoning laws, all the rooms in a home are required to receive some natural light from one or multiple windows, but this does not guarantee that the light is adequate by itself. The quantity and quality of natural light varies greatly from house to house and between individual rooms for several reasons. The way a room—or the house—is oriented, its size and shape, its dimensions and number of windows, and what it is situated next to, all affect its natural lighting.

__above__

In an attic-turned bedroom, lighting symmetry is achieved day and night with sky-lights and task lamps set at each side of the bed's headboard.

__right__

Natural light streaming through a window reflects off the mirror and makes the warmly appointed room even cozier. For less light, the shutters can be easily closed against the sun. At night, the small lamp in the corner provides ambient light for reading.

Orientation refers to the direction a room faces and is a critical component of lighting. In general, in the northern hemisphere, light from the north is cooler, whiter, and less intense than light from the south, which is why north-facing rooms are favored by artists for their studios (the reverse is true in the southern hemisphere). The cool northern light renders colors more accurately than does the light from the south, which burnishes warm tones. And from the north, intensity is more even and provides steady levels of illumination, as opposed to sharp contrasts of brightness and shadow.

left

During the day, enough natural light filters into the dining area to provide adequate lighting levels. Downlights provide supplement lighting. A fish aquarium built into the wall casts a blue tone.

A room's size and shape also have an impact on lighting. It is easy to assume that a small room needs less lighting than a large one, but that is not always the case, as the direction the room faces, its shape, and the size and positioning of its windows also affect lighting needs. A rectangular room with windows along a short width may need more lighting than a room with windows along its length. A room with a clear view receives more light than one blocked by a building, fence, or tree.

The natural light in a room or space is the starting point for making lighting plans. Although you can't alter the orientation of a home or space, you can compensate for its deficits with artificial lighting.

right

A room can be aesthetically improved with the inclusion of several different artificial lighting sources. Here a floor lamp provides general illumination and also functions as a reading light; a spot highlights the mantel's art; and a task light adds a touch of sparkle.

PLANNING THE LIGHT   A good lighting plan takes thought and consideration, and is ultimately useful only if it is flexible. That means the lighting must be able to conform to changing needs so it can be effective in a variety of situations. It should be able to illuminate all the spaces you plan on using in the room (at different intensities, if necessary) and also be adaptable if you choose to change the layout or function of the room.

To establish the patterns of illumination in a room, first evaluate the activities and tasks that will occur in the space. If it is a large room, this assessment will be more involved, as the space may have to accommodate several activities. Then consider all the wants and needs you have with respect to the lighting. For instance, is the room bright enough from its natural illumination during the day, or would you like it to be brighter—especially in a corner or cranny that natural light doesn't reach? Do you want the room to feel a certain way (warm and cozy or cool and formal, or small and intimate or large and airy) or to accommodate specific tasks (such as homework for the kids and a hobby or craft for you)? In every room, lighting can be used to highlight or accentuate decorative qualities as well as to ensure that your functional needs are met.

_left

Provide several lighting options in one room—task lighting for reading, a decorative light for show placed subtly on the coffee table, and a fireplace for ambience.

above

Highly reflective lampshades create pools of light, while the blind is half pulled to keep the sun's glare out.

above

Spot lights hung from a track highlight individual pieces of art and at the same time add general luminescence to the room.

right

Light borrowed from the adjoining room flows through the glassblock wall, while privacy is maintained.

The Essentials

When making lighting plans, remember the following:

■ If you are starting from scratch and designing and constructing a home, plan for plenty of electrical outlets in each room. This prevents overloading power outlets and eliminates the need for lots of wires or extension cords, which can cause accidents and are unsightly.

■ Locate wall switches in easily accessible spots at entrances to each room.

■ Wire individual lamps or fixtures in a room to a central switch to make them easier to control.

■ Use dimmer switches, which increase the range of effects that can be achieved with the same light and allow you to fine-tune the source of illumination to take advantage of other sources of light.

■ Use sensors or timers on lights in areas that require illumination for security, safety, or function, such as high-traffic areas that get very dark at night, entryways, or cabinets and closets.

left
Candlelight adds a romantic touch to this softly lit bedroom. Incandescent lamps create the yellowish light.

> **Develop**ing Lighting Plans

Use a basic floor plan to formulate the type of lighting required in every space. Each room needs a combination of three types of lighting: general or background illumination, focal or task lighting, and accent or decorative lighting.

General illumination is also called background or ambient lighting; it is usually the foundation of a lighting plan. It should be used to compensate for lack of natural light during the day, and it should provide uniform illumination throughout a room at night. This uniform illumination is usually provided by ceiling fixtures, but can also be created with a variety of light sources placed around a room that form overlapping pools of light, such as floor and table lamps; up-and downlights; or sidelights, sconces, and spots. While it can be dull and flat or harsh and glaring, overall general illumination should be shadowless, not accentuating anything particular about a space. Instead, it should project a sense of homogeneity in a space and be reassuring and restful. Focal or task lighting is directive—it creates a bright spot that draws our attention, tells us what to look at, or orients us toward an important element or activity center in a space. Task lighting is bright, concentrated, and directed to allow activities to be accomplished with safety and ease, such as preparing food, reading, working, or playing an instrument. However, task lighting also creates shadows around the objects in its field because of the intensity of illumination it throws off. Make sure that the shadows don't fall over the work area; situate the light source in front of or to the side of a person rather than behind him or her. Lamps with long, flexible heads, necks, or arms are usually relied upon to create this type of lighting. If shades that open at the top and bottom (as opposed to highly targeted and closed) are used, focal lighting can also supplement the general illumination in a room.

Accent or decorative lighting is any bright light directed into or onto a specific area for aesthetic rather than utilitarian effect. It is used to enhance or emphasize significant features or furnishings such as architectural elements, shelves, armoires, collections of objects, decorative accessories, and art. Accent lighting can have an unwavering focus to highlight with glamour and drama, or it can wash over a broader area, such as an entire wall or architectural element, for an emphasis that is obvious but more subtle. It can also comprise the accent itself, such as the drama and glitter provided by a chandelier or torchiere. In general, accent lighting should be at least three times brighter than the room's general lighting. Any fixture that can be trained to shine light in one specific direction can be used for this type of lighting. However, if it is too bright, the purpose of bringing nuance and contrast to a space is defeated. For this reason, it is advisable to outfit accent lights with dimmers so they can be adjusted if necessary.

It's critical to utilize all three types of lighting in a comprehensive plan.

> **Decor**ative Tricks

If a room is awkwardly proportioned, too large or small, prosaic and bland, or boring and lackluster, clever lighting can help correct some of these defects.

> **To make a ceiling look higher,** use floor or wall-mounted uplights to throw light up on the ceiling, or conceal lighting behind a cornice or cove mounted high on the walls at the perimeter of the room.

> **To make a ceiling look lower** and give a room an intimate demeanor, keep light away from the ceiling by placing wall lights fairly low and using shades or pendant fixtures with closed tops that won't throw any light back on the ceiling. Also, draw attention to items placed at a low level, such as pictures or wall hangings positioned low on the wall or groups of accessories placed on low surfaces, by lighting them from above or with a lamp standing on the surface.

> **To make a long, narrow space seem wider,** focus attention on a feature on one of the end walls, such as a window with an elegant treatment or an interesting piece of art, by highlighting the wall with a spotlight, and wash the other walls in the room with an even but less intense light.

> **To make a space seem larger,** wash opposite walls with light to make them seem farther apart. Alternatively, combine lighting with mirrors and reflective surfaces to increase the illusion of space. Use recessed cans or track-mounted spots, pointed downward, above a large wall-mounted mirror, or position lamps to be reflected in a mirror.

> **Surfaces with sheen—such as glass,** metal, tile, and gloss paint—reflect, heighten, and amplify light, while matte or textured surfaces absorb light rather than reflect it. The darker in tone, the more light is absorbed. Use matte surfaces in an overly bright room to cut the glare from too much sunlight.

> **To make a space more intimate,** use several table lamps to create a cozy glow. Make sure they have shades in colors that are warm rather than cool, such as alabaster, pearl, parchment, or ivory instead of white, so the light they cast has a mellow tone.

> **Window treatments have a huge impact** on light and can be used to manipulate the mood in a room. Translucent drapes, which filter natural light and produce a diffused effect, come in many weights and should be chosen with regard to this property. Slatted blinds offer optimum light control, ranging from total transparency to full screening, and also create dramatic patterns of light and shade when they are opened at various angles.

> **If there are several light sources** in a room and you are unhappy with the overall effect, change the bulbs, which may be too bright or too dim for their surroundings. If a fixture or lamp emits too much glare, replace its standard bulb with a reflector bulb.

> **To change the lighting in a room,** change the shades in a fixture. Translucent materials allow more light into a room, which makes it seem brighter, while darker shades can glow softly when the light is turned on, lending drama to the space.

> **To imbue a space with color,** which can create a specific mood, bathe a white wall with a washer fitted with a colored filter. Before doing so, research the psychological impact of the intended color. Yellow is a cheery hue that promotes feelings of well-being and increases efficiency. Blue is a soothing hue that calms nerves and induces sleep. Red is stimulating and dynamic and enhances the action wherever it is used. Green is a harmonious color that reminds us of nature and can be warm, refreshing, and earthy. Purple can be calming or exciting, depending on whether it leans more toward blue or red.

Color and Light

- Pale walls reflect natural light and spread it around the room. Darker, intensely colored hues absorb light and give a space a heightened sense of enclosure.

- White ceilings act as a huge reflector for natural and artificial light.

- Colors from the warm end of the spectrum—such as yellows and creams—can take the chilliness out of north light, while cooler colors—such as blues and greens—can be dazzling in direct sunlight.

- Every color changes shade under different lighting conditions throughout the day, which affects and reflects everything else in the room. Keep this in mind when choosing the hues of walls, drapes, and large pieces of furniture.

_above
By day, the kitchen is illuminated by natural light flowing in through the large skylight; by night, pendant lights provide ambient lighting.

› **The** Psychology of **Lighting**

Lighting has a dramatic psychological effect on how we perceive a space and affects how we feel when we use it.

For instance, sunny rooms that get lots of bright light are welcoming, warm, and cheery, making us feel good, while rooms that receive indirect light can be dull, lifeless, and cold, leaving us depressed. People also feel alert, energetic, and positive on a sunny day, which causes bright highlights and crisp shadows in a room, and the opposite on a dull, drab day, when there is no contrast and the environment is stagnant, boring, and uninspiring. The difference between these two days can be chalked up to variations in the quality of light; the proper illumination can provide contrasts in a room that emulate the attributes of a sunny day.

Environmental psychologists evaluate the stimuli that must be processed in a room by those using it, which is relevant to how a space should be lit. Rooms that are crowded, asymmetrical, disorderly, unconventional, or unfamiliar have a lot of stimuli and are considered high load, while rooms that are straightforward, symmetrical, conventional, familiar, and organized are less arousing and are considered low load. Tasks are gauged in the same way. Doing something demanding, such as reading a challenging book or writing a complex essay, is a high-load task, while tasks that are simple or routine, such as paying bills or cleaning the house, are low-load tasks. Lower-load tasks require higher-load settings for optimum performance, and vice versa. Lighting can be used to increase or decrease stimulation by creating an emotional setting in a room that affects the performance of tasks. In fact, the proportions of the three types of lighting—background illumination, task lighting, and accent lighting—determine the emotional content of a room.

A space lighted with a large proportion of background illumination, evenly diffused, and a small amount of focused task lighting or decorative accent lighting, is a low-contrast, low-stimulation space that is behaviorally neutral, as it is minimally stimulating. This type of environment is ideal for performing visual tasks such as reading or working. But too much diffuse light produces a boring, shadowless environment, which can evoke the type of bland psychological reaction experienced on a cloudy day.

A space lighted with a small amount of diffuse light and a larger amount of focal light is a high-contrast environment featuring strong patterns of light and shade. This type of lighting plan increases stimulation and is intended to evoke specific moods and emotions. A room lit in this manner can also dominate the people in it; the contrast produces visual direction and focus by directing their attention and holding their interest.

Overall, people need lower-loaded settings for difficult, complex tasks or to feel contented, comfortable, and relaxed, and higher-loaded spaces for casual, pleasant activities or socializing, as a high degree of contrast encourages participation and stimulates enjoyment.

Light strings, so essential for a festive mood during the holidays, can be fun any time of the year and may be just the thing to liven up a theme party. Medium-weight papers will hold their shape when folded, but are still thin enough to let light shine through. Personalize your shades for any kind of party using specialty punches like the sun we used, and different paper edgers. You can also try lining your shades with white or colored vellum for a softer light through the punches.

Punched Paper Light String

Materials

- Light string
- Star and sun paper punches
- One large sheet (about 19 inch x 25 inch [48 cm x 64 cm]) of medium-weight art paper, such as pastel paper, of each of the following colors: red, yellow, and orange
- Double-stick tape
- Ruler
- Pencil
- Scissors or a craft knife
- Deckle edge paper edgers

TIP Make a sample lantern and see if you like the size in relation to your light string. Some light strings may have close-together lights that will look better with smaller shades; simply reduce the panel height and width proportionately to make a smaller shade.

1. Measure and cut paper for lanterns.

From one of the colors, using the ruler and pencil, measure and mark a 6-inch-tall by 12 1/2-inch-wide (15 cm x 32 cm) piece of paper; repeat three times for a total of four panels. From the other two colors, measure and cut three panels each.

2. Fold lanterns.

Using the ruler, measure up 2 1/2 inches (6 cm) from one of the long edges, and draw a line from short edge to short edge; then mark a line 1 3/4 inch (4 cm) up from the same edge. Place the ruler on the 2 1/2 inch (6 cm) mark and fold the paper up along it, then remove the ruler and make a sharper fold. Do not fold along the other line. Repeat for all the panels of paper.

Next, fold each panel into fifths, using the ruler and technique described above, each section should be 2 1/2 inch wide (6 cm). Make each fold in the same direction to form the shade.

Make flaps for the shade by cutting along the creases that have divided the shade into fifths, starting at the longer edge of the paper where you measured up 2 1/2 inch (6 cm) to begin with, and stopping once you get to the horizontal fold. Using the previously marked line 1 3/4 inch (4 cm) from the edge of the paper that you didn't fold as a guide, trim the first, third, and fifth flaps; they should measure 3/4 inch (2 cm).

Punch a random design in the second, third, and fourth sections at this point.

3. Fold lanterns and finish the shades.

Bring the first and last panels together and align them; secure with double-stick tape rather than glue to avoid warping the shades.

Punch the fourth side of the shades. Then, gently flatten each shade and trim the edge with the paper edgers.

4. Attach shades to the light string.

Place a light in between the short flaps of one of the shades, then fold the two longer flaps over the string and each other; secure with double-stick tape.

Handmade paper, available in a variety of styles and colors to match your taste and home, is even more appealing when combined with pressed leaves or flowers. This hurricane, which can be assembled in under an hour, can be easily adjusted to fit the decor of any room. Be sure to test the translucency of the paper you select by holding it up to the light. You can apply this technique to any glass container you want, or use bits of torn paper rather than a whole piece to cover the container for a mosaic or collage feel.

Leaf and Paper Hurricane

Materials
- Glass container, such as a cylindrical or square vase, or a hurricane shade
- Several pressed leaves or flowers
- Thin, handmade paper
- Ruler
- Pencil
- All-in-one découpage glue, sealer, and finish such as Aleene's gloss finish
- Foam applicator brush

TIP You can press your own leaves in a telephone book until dry, approximately one or two weeks, depending on humidity. Many craft stores offer skeletonized leaves, which have been treated so that only the veins and stem remain, resulting in a subtle, ethereal effect.

For easier lighting and the best effect, choose a candle that is about half as tall as the container.

1. Measure and cut the paper.
Place the glass container on the paper, and wrap the paper around it. As you wrap, mark a line for cutting with a pencil along the edges of the container at the top and bottom. Then unwrap the container, and add 1/4 inch (.5 cm) to the length for the seam. Next, tear the paper by laying a ruler along your marks and gently pulling the paper toward you. The irregular edges will produce a softer look and will help disguise the seam.

2. Arrange the pressed leaves or flowers.
Clean and dry the container. Apply a thin, even coat of glue on the vase where you want the leaves or flowers to be, using sponge applicator. Arrange them as desired, and gently smooth the leaves outward from the stem with the sponge applicator. Be sure there are no wrinkles or air bubbles in the leaves. For brittle but thick foliage, gently coat the back with glue first, which will make it more pliable.

3. Apply the paper to the vase.
Gently apply a thin, even coat of glue to the entire container, including the leaves or flowers. Position one edge of the paper on the container where you want the seam to be and begin wrapping it on smoothly and slowly. Smooth out wrinkles and bubbles as you go along. Finally, apply another thin, even coat of glue over the paper and let it dry overnight before using.

Lighting Living Areas

In every room in a home, there is a constant give and take between natural and artificial light. This ever-changing dynamic unfolds over the course of an entire day and night. Thus, the features of a room—such as its dimensions and architectural details; the size, type, and number of its windows; its orientation to the world outside; and the way it is used throughout the day—are all key elements that must be considered from sunup to sundown when lighting that room. Ultimately, it is important to pay as much attention to the effect sunlight has in that room as it is to consider the impact that artificial lights have in the same space.

Few of us realize all this when setting out to light our living areas. Traditionally, a standard-issue lighting plan has evolved for each of the public spaces in our homes. The living room contains several seating or activity areas, as it is a multipurpose space for most of us, and these are generally lit with floor lamps. An additional form of general illumination is usually present overhead, either in the form of tracks, a central ceiling fixture, or recessed cans. In dining areas, the dramatic pendant fixture or chandelier reigns supreme. In bedrooms, the bed or an easy chair off to one side is usually flanked with reading lamps, while the entire room is illuminated with a ceiling fixture. While this standard approach is tempting, it is not the most effective way to light a room.

left
A simple table lamp supplements a living room's ambient lighting while also serving a decorative purpose.

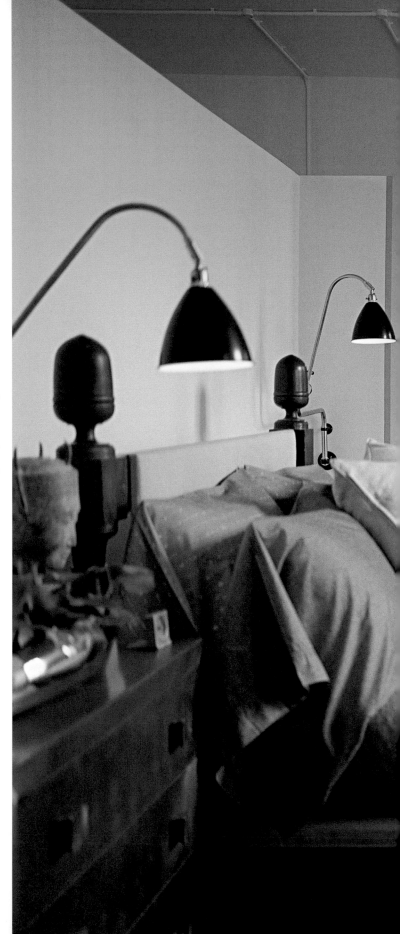

In a perfect world, we would be able to address the lighting needs of a room before it is furnished, or even while its blueprints are still in on the drawing board, but in reality, it is impossible for most of us to start from scratch. We move in and out of residences with more frequency than ever before, sometimes physically altering them by installing the sort of lighting we need when we get there. Often, we address immediate lighting needs with store-bought fixtures, yet carefully planned alterations to lighting at any stage can radically improve a room from both a functional and an aesthetic perspective. When those rooms are the ones we use most of the time, these changes become even more meaningful.

right
When the daylight fads, a hierarchy of artificial lighting takes over—ranging from the two clip-on task lights over the bed pillows to the focused desk lamp to the long-armed flexible floor lamp to the romantic glow of the fire.

LIGHTING PUBLIC LIVING SPACES Today, we often spend the bulk of our time in open, airy rooms used for a variety of activities, such as relaxing, watching television, reading, listening to music, and entertaining friends, or even working on hobbies, homework, or special projects. We refer to these spaces with an assortment of terms, such as great room, family room, den, or even the plain, old-fashioned-term living room, but in essence, they are hardworking, multipurpose spaces that have to accommodate a range of disparate endeavors.

Just as lighting draws attention to actors on a stage, it must highlight and accommodate the various parts of the set in these sorts of rooms. At the same time, the lighting must play up the room's best assets. It is necessary to focus adequate amounts of the right kind of light on various furniture groupings and, at the same time, complement and enhance the decor of the room. Reconciling these needs requires a combination of the three types of lighting (namely, general, task, and accent lighting (see Developing Lighting Plans in Chapter 1).

above
A contemporary floor lamp complements one of a pair of sconces to more than adequately light this living space.

right
By day, natural light heightens the color of this traditional drawing room. At night, the yellow walls, lit by an overhead fixture and two table lamps, mellow and a burning fire brings a gentleness to the room.

In dining areas, or those portions of multipurpose spaces that are used for dining, the chandelier is still the fixture of choice—for good reason. Not only is it a suitable and often even superior source of light, it is an exceptional decorative asset that can go a long way toward expressing the specific style of a room. A frothy crystal version adds elegance and grandeur to a space, while a rustic wrought-iron fixture can convey intimacy and warmth. Today, pendant fixtures are available in a broad range of styles and are used with the same frequency as the chandelier.

It is important to keep several considerations in mind when selecting a hanging fixture for a dining area. The fixture should complement the size and shape of the dining table as well as the decor of the room. Before electricity was commonplace, such lamps were fitted with candles and hung high over a table to eliminate the danger of fire, but now, a hanging fixture should be suspended about 30 inches (762 millimeters) above the table. If the fixture has an open shade and bare bulbs, it should be suspended as high as necessary to avoid a harsh glare in diners' eyes, or a bulb with a silvered crown should be used to reduce glare. Also, the diameter of a hanging light should be at least a foot shorter than the table below it, and when the ceiling height is over 8 feet (2.4 meters), balance the space by raising the fixture 3 inches (76.2 millimeters) for every additional foot of ceiling space. Tame dramatic but too-dazzling pendant fixtures and chandeliers with a dimmer control. Finally, remember that no rule dictates the use of a hanging fixture. Recessed cans or tracks equipped with downlights can also be used to adequately light a dining table, which can be accented with flickering candles to change the ambience or mood.

above
The chandelier's motif is reflected in the flower arrangement on the table below.

left
Modern-day chandeliers come in unusual shapes and forms.

LIGHTING PRIVATE LIVING SPACE Gone are the days when bedrooms were meant solely for sleep. Today, they have become multi-purpose rooms and/or private sanctuaries for many members of the family. Sometimes, bedrooms are even entire suites that span several rooms for those lucky enough to have such space at their disposal. All this makes the lighting requirements in our bedrooms as varied and complex as any other living space in the home.

Just consider all the activities that take place in this room, from reading, writing and watching television to rummaging around for what to wear and dressing. All these activities, save sleeping, requires a specific source of light, and if two people are sharing the space, it calls for sources of light that are flexible enough to be adjusted to two activities at once. For instance, if one person wants to read or must get dressed while the other is sleeping, the lighting in the room should be deftly planned to accommodate such subtle or specialized adjustments. All this reinforces the idea that a bedroom needs both general illumination and task lighting. Often, accent lighting also comes into play as a decorative element.

above
A wispy chandelier marks the center of this living room bringing sparkle lights at night.

right
The lighting of a bedroom dresser takes a more personal touch with lamps that provide ambient lighting but also a touch of whimsy.

So where to start? In fact, the traditional ceiling hung or mounted fixture is entirely inappropriate in the bedroom for many reasons. In this particular room, points of activity tend to be situated around the perimeter of the room rather than anchored in the center. Beds are usually positioned against walls rather than in the center of a bedroom; a reading area is often incorporated into the bed set-up with task lighting or sequestered in intimate corners with the aid of easy chairs and lamps; and dressers or bureaus are also placed against walls. All this necessitates lighting sources that are tied to the layout of the room and the needs of its users. Also, if there are translucent shades or drapes in a bedroom, ceiling mounted fixtures can unwittingly silhouette intimate moments.

Ultimately, because of the nature of the bedroom and its most important activity, namely sleeping, this is one area of the home where flexibility is paramount. So it pays to increase the variability of light sources in the space by outfitting them all with dimmer switches. To read in bed, besides typical bedside lamps, swing-arm fixtures can be mounted to the wall, or for the most maneuverability, affixed directly to the bedpost with screw-tightened vises so they can ride up and down for the best positioning. Or consider spotlights or reading lamps on clips that can be used on a headboard or bedframe. And finally, don't forget to have two main light switches in the room: one by the door and one by the bed, since there is nothing more irritating than getting out of bed when you're almost asleep to turn off the lights.

_left
Double task lamps attractively provide more than adequate reading light in a spot where occupants often complain there is not enough.

Fixture Formulas

To get the most out of a fixture, position it optimally with regard to its purpose. For instance, a pendant fixture intended to provide ambient or background illumination casts a broader path of light the closer it is to the ceiling, but if it is meant to provide task lighting, it must be set lower. Here are guidelines to follow:

- Lamps used for reading: Both floor lamps and table lamps next to chairs have the same requirements. The bottom of the shade should be about 40 inches (1,101.6 millimeters) to 42 inches (1,066.8 millimeters) above the floor, which is slightly below eye level for a seated reader of average height. Lamps behind chairs should be taller; the distance from the floor to the base of the shade should be a minimum of 47 inches (1,193.8 millimeters). The lamp should be placed approximately 10 inches (254 millimeters) behind the shoulder of the reader. Next to beds, the base of a lampshade should be 20 inches (508 millimeters) above the pillow.

- Task lighting: The height of fixtures and lamps varies by task, but rules of thumb are available. A pendant fixture should be about 30 inches (762 millimeters) above the top of a dining table, but if a room is over 8 feet tall (2.4 meters tall), add 3 inches per foot above 8 feet to this figure. Light sources used for light-intensive tasks, such as working, writing, sewing, drawing, or working with tools, should be 14 inches to 15 inches (355.6 millimeters to 381 millimeters) above the center of the work, which should be positioned 10 inches to 14 inches (254 millimeters to 355.6 millimeters) in front of the worker.

- Wall-mounted fixtures: Heights vary and depend on the way the fixture is designed and the height and size of the wall, but, in general, they should be placed above eye level. They should also be fairly flat, not protruding more than 4 inches (101.6 millimeters) from a wall, unless they are placed well above the level where they can be bumped by heads (which is at least 80 inches {2,032 millimeters} above the floor).

- Track lighting: The beauty of this type of lighting is its flexibility; the fixtures can be moved along the track to where they are needed and positioned at any angle to become a downlight, spotlight, or accent light for art and collectibles. To accent an item on a wall, position the fixtures at a 30-degree angle.

right

The light from two column torchieres is doubled as it bounces off full height mirrors in the library-music room. Swirly decorative torches holding candles flank the fireplace and add a modern romantic touch.

above

The lava lamp, which provides great ambient lighting, is making a comeback.

right

Three pendants mark the dining area in this family room.

right

A cascading chandelier highlights the dining area, while a funky floor lamp provides reading light in the sitting room.

> **Plan**ning Points

Consider the following points when planning a lighting scheme for a room:

> Activities: What will be happening in the room, and where will each specific action take place?

> Highlights: What features in the room need emphasis? Stunning architectural elements, such as magnificent mantels or intricate ceilings, should be bathed in light to show them off.

> Deficits: What needs to be concealed? Faults, such as ugly architectural ornamentation or badly plastered walls, should not be emphasized with light.

> Ambience: What is the desired mood for the room? Dramatic or soothing? Businesslike or cheery and bright? The choice dictates the intensity and positioning of the light sources in the room.

> Balance: Should the entire room be brightly lit, or would pockets of brightness and shadow be desirable? If the latter, make sure these pockets balance each other and do not detract from the room's functionality.

> Flexibility: To accommodate different activities in the room, make sure the level of general illumination is adequate and employ free-standing fixtures that can be moved at will.

> Variety: A lighting plan that uses all the same fixtures or lamps can be both boring and inadequate, as it is unlikely that one type of item can satisfy all requirements. Use a diversity of light sources in a room, and choose attractive and creative options.

> Decorative style: Make sure the light sources complement or match the decorative style of a room. If a light source is particularly stunning in itself, such as an intricate chandelier or an artist-made lamp, it can even be the focal point of the space.

> **Find**ing the Right Fixtures

A good lighting plan is only the beginning of the process to follow when lighting a home. After identifying the lighting requirements of a room, the next step is to fulfill them. This often calls for employing all three types of lighting in a space (see Developing Lighting Plans in Chapter 1), and it also takes careful planning. At times, it may even demand a bit of experimentation.

Once you know the types of illumination needed in a room, it is possible to select fixtures and lamps. While it isn't necessary to master the complex calculations of the professional designer, a working familiarity with the different types of lights and fixtures is helpful in making an informed choice. Consider the quality of light each fixture gives off, its aesthetic appearance, how sturdy it is, and the type of light it emits (see sidebar, "Types of Light"). Also, keep in mind that no light can serve every purpose or meet every need.

Lighting fixtures come in every form, shape, size, and style imaginable, and are made of myriad materials. In fact, the possibilities are endless, and there is no such thing as one right choice. However, all these options boil down to three general categories and, when lighting a space, it is usually necessary to choose fixtures from each of these groups to create schemes that balance function with aesthetics.

> Freestanding Fixtures

This type of lighting can range from soaring torchieres to squat table lamps. Sometimes freestanding fixtures are stunning works of art in their own right. Basically, however, they can be used to address every lighting need, depending on the style and properties of the particular lamp. Torchieres are uplights, which can be used to create ambient light, while floor and table lamps usually sport shades that suit them for focal or task lighting. Freestanding fixtures have the flexibility to be moved wherever you need them and don't have complex installation requirements; you merely plug them in. There are two basic types of freestanding lamps: uplights and lamps with shades. (The term lamp is usually used to refer to freestanding fixtures but, technically, a lamp is the part of a bulb that emits light.)

Uplights work best in rooms with high ceilings, where they make an ideal source for general illumination. Uplights can use the ceiling as a giant reflector to create a softly diffused ambient light in a space, provided the ceiling is painted white or a light color (dark colors absorb light). The height of an uplight determines the intensity and quality of the light it yields as it reflects off the ceiling; those close to the ceiling produce a concentrated light, while those that are lower produce light that is softly diffused. In general, the greater the distance between the uplight and the ceiling, the greater the area illuminated.

Lamps usually consist of a base or stand that supports a socket, the bulb, and a shade. The power cord is concealed by the base, and the shape and substance of the shade determine the quality and quantity of light the lamp emits. The beauty and versatility of the lamp lie in this simple design, for the base and shade can be made of myriad materials, take virtually any form, and be rendered in any decorative style. Also, the shade can direct the light of the bulb in any direction, though most focus the light downward to create a softly diffused pool of illumination. The wider the shade, the broader the pool of illumination.

above
A pyramid-shaped floor lamp with tapered linen shade.

A clip-on spot provides convenient lighting for artwork.

> **Ceiling Fixtures**

Illumination from above is one of the most basic ways to light a room, and depending on how they are installed and the intensity of the bulbs, ceiling fixtures can provide background or general illumination in a room as well as task and accent lighting. There are many ways to mount fixtures on the ceiling, and basic ceiling fixtures are usually made of translucent glass, sport simple curved or geometric shapes, and are attached to, rather than hung from, the ceiling. Either one or several fixtures are used to provide general illumination in a room. They are also usually used in high-traffic areas, such as hallways, kitchens, and bathrooms, especially when ceiling heights are low. Five types of ceiling fixtures offer specialized and directed lighting options: pendants, chandeliers, downlights, spotlights, and tracks.

Pendants hang from the ceiling and can be used to provide general or task illumination, depending on how they are finished off. The bulb can be covered with translucent globes for diffused ambient illumination that radiates throughout the room, or trained in a specific direction with shaped shades for task lighting. Small pendants can be used at various points in a room, or even grouped together, for more illumination and for their combined decorative effect. They can be all the same or related in terms of color or styling.

Chandeliers, which are pendants with branches that hold bulbs (or,

in some cases, candles) as well as decorative ornamentation, are the most dramatic type of ceiling fixture. The quality of light produced varies with the number, type, and strength of the bulbs, the style of the fixture (some have many branches or sport individual shades over each bulb), and whether or not the fixture is equipped with a dimmer. A chandelier is the focal point of the space or room it occupies and must be chosen accordingly.

Downlights are minimal ceiling fixtures that are inconspicuously mounted on or in the ceiling to cast light directly down on a surface. They can be surface mounted, recessed, partially recessed, and used to provide all three types of lighting, but are particularly effective at focal illumination. The beam of light downlights emit can vary in width, depending on the shape of the fixture and type of bulb that is used; recessed lighting produces the narrowest beam. Downlights are often used over work counters for task lighting, or to accent or emphasize a particular area or feature of a room. While they are ideal for low ceilings where pendant lights would be unsuitable, fully recessed lighting requires a half-foot of space above the ceiling to accommodate the fixture and provide proper ventilation.

Spotlights, like downlights, are minimal fixtures that are available in a wide variety of shapes and styles, but they are extremely adjustable and are used to focus on, or emphasize, specific spots in a space. They can be installed or mounted on walls, floors, ceilings, or standing polls, set in

tracks, or used individually with clips for greatest flexibility. They are best for accent lighting, as the bulb and fixture are designed to work together to give a precise, controlled beam of light that can be tilted, swiveled, or angled to wherever it is needed. However, in large, open spaces, spotlights can be used for general illumination by positioning them to create overlapping pools of light. This technique produces ambient lighting that is a bit more interesting than the uniform level of illumination provided by basic ceiling and pendant fixtures.

Track lighting is often referred to as its own type of lighting, but it is actually a combination of spotlights and downlights installed in a flexible arrangement on a ceiling-mounted track. Track lighting can be used for general, task, and accent lighting because it is possible to swivel, rotate, or point the individual fixtures in any direction; often, the same track incorporates all three types of illumination. Track lighting comes in two forms. Some tracks are fixed and come with specific light fixtures already attached, while others are merely free-form power lines that can be used to anchor a number of types of fixtures along its length.

> Wall-Mounted Fixtures

Like ceilings, walls provide a functional and accessible surface for mounting fixtures, and, like lamps, fixtures designed to be wall-mounted come in a tremendous scope of styles ranging from period or traditional versions to cutting-edge designs. Some emit an all-round glow, such as those encased in glass globes or translucent lanterns, while others train lights either up, down, or at a specific spot due to the way they are shaped. In most cases, these fixtures are in harmony with the walls they grace, using the surface as a reflective plane to create a subtle source of ambient light in a room. Unlike ceiling lights, which usually generate a steady level of light in a room, wall lights can be used to create pockets of light or dramatic ebbs and flows in a room.

Sconces are a common form of wall-mounted lighting; they were once ornamental wall brackets meant to hold candles, but they hold electric bulbs today. Some sconce styles take candle-shaped bulbs. When such bulbs are left exposed, opt for lower wattage to avoid glare. Sconces are often used in pairs and, depending on their design, become a focal point when employed in this way. They can also instill a sense of symmetry and drama in a setting when used to surround a piece of furniture, such as a bureau or bed, or an architectural element, such as a mantel or a doorway.

Wall washers, another form of wall-mounted lighting, are usually installed at the top of a wall, pointing down, to bathe the walls with a steady, uniform, and soft level of illumination. With these fixtures, the results are most effective when the wall is smooth and painted a light color to maximize its reflective properties.

above
Add this sconce and cord cover without drilling a hole in your wall.

> **Balanc**ing Acts

The lighting fixtures that are used should be balanced in terms of the furnishings that surround them, whether sofas and tables or other sources of light. They should also match or complement the style of the decor in a home. Keep these points in mind:

> **Lighting fixtures** placed near each other should be balanced in terms of weight and the amount of light they emit. For instance, a very tall lamp placed next to a short lamp overwhelms it, and the light emitted by both lamps is uneven and perhaps even conflicting. The same is true of wall sconces, which should be kept consistent in style and light emission throughout a room, especially if they bracket an architectural or decorative element such as a fireplace, mirror, bureau, or doorway.

> **Relate the scale** of a fixture or lamp to the scale of the furnishings that surround it rather than the scale of the room. If a small space is filled with a chunky sofa, pair it with a chunky table lamp with a wide shade. Hang a husky pendant lamp over a burly, masculine dining table; pair a curvy, delicate sofa with a like-minded table lamp or floor lamp; use weighty sconces to surround a massive stone hearth.

> **Stay within the parameters** of a room's decor. If the style has a country demeanor, use lamps made of down-home materials such as earthenware crocks and mason jars. In a formal milieu, stick to prim and proper fixtures in elegant materials with graceful shades. In a period room, such as one with art deco or modernist furnishings, use vintage or reproduction pieces that approximate or imitate the style.

> **When a fixture** is paired with an important piece of furniture in a room, it should relate to the piece. Complement a contemporary glass or marble dining table with a fixture that echoes its shape or the materials used to fabricate it. For instance, pair a round glass table with a round glass pendant, or repeat a geometric motif in the fixture over a square marble-topped table. Surround a lacquered oriental armoire with lantern-style sconces.

> **Be sure to bring** decorative details and incidental furnishings into play when possible. Match the color or pattern of textiles in a room with shades in the same colors or motifs, or use the same trim from pillows or drapes to edge shades. Surround a gilt-framed mirror with gilt sconces, reflect wrought-iron curtain rods with a wrought-iron chandelier, or get a fixture with a stainless-steel shade to complement stainless-steel kitchen counters.

above

Matching geometric-shaped table lamps flank the sofa and reflect the décor's stylistic leanings. The decorative lamp atop the cabinet adds delight as well as light.

The simple appeal of a Japanese-styled lantern can add a clean, modern look to a bedroom or dining table. With simple supplies and elegant, authentic Japanese paper, you can create a lantern of your own without a hammer and nails. Craft and hobby wood, such as balsa or basswood, works best because it is very soft and easy to cut. For a more traditional look, divide the panels into evenly-spaced multiple panes.

Japanese Table Lantern

Materials

- All-purpose clear-drying glue
- Balsa or basswood strips: four 1/2-inch-wide (1 cm) strips, and four 1/4-inch-wide (.5 cm) strips (these are available at hobby and craft stores and come in approximately 24-inch-long (61 cm) strips)
- Thin piece of plywood, no less than 1/8 inch (.3 cm) thick but no more than 1/4 inch (.5cm) (small pieces are also are available at hobby and craft stores)
- Thin, handmade rice paper or something similar
- White cardstock that matches the rice paper
- Light-colored wood stain and finish in one
- Sponge brush applicator
- Ruler
- Pencil
- Craft knife
- Hobby saw attachment for craft knives
- Gridded cutting mat
- Fine sandpaper

TIP Use a cotton swab to apply small amounts of glue precisely and evenly. Use sandpaper to make the lantern's legs level and steady.

1. Measure and cut the wood.

From the 1/2-inch-wide (1 cm) strips, cut eight 12-inch-long (30 cm) strips using the hobby saw. From the 1/4-inch- wide (.5 cm) strips, cut eight 5 inch (13 cm) strips, eight 2 3/8 inch (6 cm) strips, and four 9 1/2 inch (24 cm) strips using the hobby saw. Cut the plywood to be 6 inch (15 cm) square using the hobby saw.

2. Measure and cut the paper.

Using a craft knife and a gridded cutting mat, cut four pieces of paper 6 inches wide by 10 inches tall (15 cm x 25 cm). Make sure that each piece is exactly the same size, and properly squared up.

To make reinforcements for the corners of the lantern, cut four 1/2 inch wide by 9 7/8 inches (1 cm x 25 cm) long strips from the white cardstock. Then, measure in 1/4 inch (.5 cm) and lightly score them with the craft knife down the length; fold the paper to make a 90 degree angle. From the rice paper, also cut four 1/2-inch-wide by 9 7/8-inch-long (1 cm x 25 cm) strips and glue them into the corners; they do not need to be scored because the paper is very thin and easily folded.

Also make reinforcements for the inside bottom of the lantern where the panels meet the base of the lantern by repeating the above technique; make four more reinforcements 5 7/8 inch long (15 cm).

3. Assemble the four panels of the lantern.

To assemble each panel, lay a piece of paper on the gridded mat and glue a 1/2 inch-wide (1 cm) piece of wood, flush with the edge of the paper, to both long sides with 1 inch (3 cm) extending above and below. Use the mat's markings to be sure the wood is properly aligned with the paper.

Next, glue a 5 inch (13 cm) strip to the top and bottom shorter edges of the panel, flush with the edge of the paper. Be sure to add a dab of glue to each end of the strips as well. Then glue a 9 1/2 inch (24 cm) strip to the center of the panel. Finally, add a 2 3/8 inch (6 cm) strip down 3 inches from the top strip on the left side of the middle strip, and another 2 3/8 inch (6 cm) strip up 3 inches from the bottom strip on the right side of the middle strip.

4. Assemble the lantern.

Once all the panels have dried, glue each to one side of the 6 inch (15 cm) square base, aligning the bottom edge of the base with the bottom edge of the paper; use glue only at this point. Wait for the glue to set, but not dry completely before going on to the adjacent side. Glue the reinforcements in place as you create the side and bottom corners.

Papyrus, with it's tartan-like weave, adds visual interest to a simple shade and sheds a warm, soft glow. A papyrus shade paired with a reclaimed treasure from your attic or a yard sale makes a unique and personal accent for any room. Bottles are easiest to convert to a lamp base, but with a little extra effort, you can transform just about anything. Once you've assembled one lamp, you'll see how easy it is to make one from anything, such as a vase, pitcher, or ceramic crock.

Papyrus Shade Lamp

Materials

- A container to convert to the lamp bottom, such as the antique seltzer bottle seen here
- Self-adhesive lamp shade in a size appropriate for the base
- A large sheet of papyrus
- One package of 1/4 inch (.5 cm) double fold bias binding, off-white
- Wiring and lamp hardware kit for bottles (available at hardware stores)
- Fabric glue
- Scissors

TIP When selecting paper for a shade, always check what it will look like when backed by a light bulb and a layer of thick white paper, to simulate the shade backing. Thicker papers may not diffuse the light enough, and the patterns of very thin papers may be washed out. To make the pattern of a thinner paper show up better, try gluing it to a piece of thick white paper with spray adhesive, then attaching it to the shade.

1. Cut the paper for the shade.
Tape the paper to your work surface, and trace the shape of the lampshade wrapper on the paper with a pencil. Cut the paper along this line.

2. Attach the paper to the shade.
Starting at the seam, wrap the shade with the paper. Use the fabric glue to secure the seam.

3. Add the trim.
Before cutting the trim, tape one end to the top of the shade and wrap it around to see how much you will need. Cut at this point, then repeat to measure the amount needed for the bottom of the shade. Using fabric glue, secure the trim to the edges of the shade, inside and out.

4. Assemble the lamp hardware and fit it to the base.
Many hardware stores have kits for wiring bottles that contain several sizes of gaskets for fitting the lamp hardware into the bottle's opening, and the cords are designed to come straight out at the socket rather than down into the bottle. This allows you to preserve the look of the transparent container.

Following the kit's instructions, attach the cord to the socket. Then attach the "harp" to the socket. The harp is what the lampshade will attach to; a taller harp will show more of the base, and a shorter harp will conceal some of it. Using a finial, and washers for a tight fit (if necessary), attach the shade.

If you choose a bottom that has a larger opening than a bottle, such as an antique vase, the assembly will be virtually the same, but you will need to get the proper hardware from an electrical or lighting supply store, or from a mail-order source.

Lighting Hardworking Areas

Bright, concentrated light is an essential ingredient in the hardworking areas of a home. It keeps us alert, focused, and even safe at what can sometimes be hazardous tasks, such as cutting vegetables with sharp knives. Task lighting is therefore the choice for areas where concentrated activities repeatedly occur—in the home office or study, the kitchen, the bathroom.

Task lighting, be it a table lamp or a focused, recessed light, casts a bright directional beam on a defined area, yet achieving visual comfort in hardworking areas demands accurate placement of the light as well as merely selecting the fixture. The light should be positioned to avoid excessive glare, reflectance, and shadows. What use is task lighting if you are working in your own shadow or if the light bounces off a polished surface nearby and the excessive glare bothers you?

left
With lighting fixtures strategically placed, this well-lit bathroom becomes a shimmering sanctuary, where simple lines and colors are used.

To understand this concept, think of the structure of the human eye. The pupil automatically enlarges or contracts to admit more or less light. Alternating excessive and limited light levels tires the eye muscles. Therefore, bright task lighting in an otherwise dim room is counterproductive. Your attention doesn't always stay on the task but wanders into the darker surroundings. Ambient lighting and natural lighting should balance the hardworking area to diminish eye fatigue. A balanced combination of lighting also offers a psychologically gentler environment in which to work and a more aesthetically pleasing room.

The most common hardworking areas are the kitchen, home office or study, and bathroom. A corner of the living room, however, can be turned into a workspace by installing a desk and computer. A garage or basement can be a carpenter's haven. The following discussion addresses the first three generic spaces but offers suggestions that can apply to your home's own hardworking areas.

THE KITCHEN The hardest-working area in most homes, the kitchen, is where we store, prepare, and cook food daily. In addition, it's often where the family congregates for casual conversations or for meals. Lighting needs, therefore, include both task and ambient applications. In the food preparation area, the lighting plan is largely fixed due to the permanence of cabinets and appliances. Safety is a major consideration and effective task lighting is essential where sharp implements are used, water is boiled, gas is fired, and electric rings glow. An unnecessary shadow or moment of glare can cause injury. Further, the color the light casts significantly affects our perception of the food we are preparing.

___**above**
A creative use of task lamps in the kitchen.

___**left**
No sleepy souls in this highly reflective stainless steel kitchen. Because of the surface reflectivity, a little light goes a long way and there are obvious and hidden light sources throughout the room.

The limitations in the kitchen also provide excellent solutions. In the prep area, freestanding lights and pendants can be obtrusive but downlights, recessed lights, and lights mounted on the lower surfaces of cabinets are often ideal for task lighting. These lights should be positioned towards the front edges of cabinetry rather than the back, since bulbs placed towards the rear of a cabinet will reflect off the wall and may not reach the part of the counter where tasks are executed. However, lights too far forward can also cause your body or arms to cast shadows on the work at hand, which can compromise safety. So it is important to get the positioning of these lights right, and it often calls for old-fashioned trial and error.

above
Although adequate natural light flows through the clerestory, the placement of spots under the cabinets for task lighting and the pendant light provide necessary supplement illumination.

right
A band of clerestory windows allows natural light to flow into the kitchen. Artificial lighting from pendants, under cabinet spots and a fluorescent strip takes over when the natural lighting dims.

Concealed Lighting

Task lighting in kitchens demonstrates a decorative trick that can be used elsewhere in the home to dramatic effect—concealing the light source. Take this concept of concealed lighting from the kitchen to other rooms in the house. It's particularly useful for overhead lights and where special shelving display opportunities exist. Use your imagination to identify unlikely places to recess lights. Your task is made easier because of the wide range of bulbs and fixtures that can be used as concealed lighting—incandescent and fluorescent alike.

- Run a strip of fluorescent or halogen lights underneath cabinets or shelves to illuminate a work area.

- Place spotlights underneath cabinets and over work or preparation areas in any room to bring shadowless light to detailed work.

- Use the top of the cabinets or shelves, or even a large piece of furniture such as an armoire, for a run of lights. These reflect off the ceiling to produce a great deal of ambient light.

- Install automatic lights inside cabinets or closets that switch on when the doors are opened.

- Place a light strip underneath a shelf to illuminate the objects below it.

Over cook tops or stoves, lights can be installed under exhaust hoods or on the ceiling, either recessed or mounted on a track and pointed at the work area. Sinks and drain boards also need to be well lit, even if this seems unnecessary because they are ofttimes situated in front of large windows. But it is important to be able to see if dishes are clean, or target the spot where boiling water will be drained, and when it's cloudy there must be enough illumination to compensate for the lack of natural light. Also keep in mind that high gloss surfaces, such as stainless steel or tiles, can cause glare, while dark materials, such as granite or slate, will absorb light so more fixtures or higher wattage bulbs may be necessary.

While pendants are not suitable as task lighting, they can work as a source of general illumination when they are astutely chosen and installed, such as a series of fixtures hanging in a row, calculated to be at the right height to avoid getting in the way. Or, they can add a decorative dimension to eating areas, particularly when the dining table is separated from the prep counter. And for ambient lighting, try tube lights concealed behind the moldings at the top of wall cabinets to wash the ceiling with light.

above

A track configuration—called a color monorail— brings flexibility and visual interest to this kitchen. Additional lighting is provided by cabinet uplights.

below

Taking full advantage of all lighting opportunities— notice the pendants, cabinet up and downlights, ceiling downlights, and even the lights placed underneath the fireplace's hood.

above
A flexible working lamp for a flexible working space.

left
A corner of a bedroom can serve as an office, particularly when task lighting designates the workspace, but also when the opportunity for natural light is offered as a relief for the user.

THE HOME OFFICE/STUDY The home computer has become a ubiquitous feature of the American household. Whether setting up a home office or simply turning a corner of the living room into a work area, the computer needs a permanent space. The user needs to comfortably see the keyboard, screen, and notes on the desk alongside. Task lighting—a concentrated pool of light—is essential, but tricky. The task light should be angled to fall on the keyboard, not the screen. At the same time, the light should fall on the sheet of paper without producing glare. The light source itself should not shine in the user's eyes but be protected from view.

Fortunately, task lighting with flexible arms and heads that can be adjusted from a tight, close focus to a more diffuse illumination is available. The most effective task lighting usually takes the form of a flexible desk lamp, which has the advantage of being totally adjustable. It should be able to rotate, bend, swivel or turn to throw light wherever it is most needed. The best known example of this is the standard Anglepoise desk lamp, which is a lamp with a long, bendable jointed arm that comes in myriad variations. Some have heavy bases, while others clip or clamp onto a surface to anchor their arms. Still other directional lamps are flexible thanks to sliding or hinged arms, moving joints, flexible stems, or adjustable shades. With these options, as you move, the light can move with you.

It is also important to correctly position directional task lighting so you avoid working in your own shadow. To do so, place lamps at the opposite side of the work surface from your dominant hand and far enough away do that the light falls across the work surface diagonally from the top left or right (depending on which of your hands is dominant). Also make sure that no light shines directly on a computer screen, which will cause an irritating glare. Direct sunlight can also interfere with the computer screen; the answer is to angle the screen away from the window, and invest in a translucent blind or sheer curtain to filter the sun's rays without blocking them out.

Don't count on task lighting satisfying all your needs, or you will fatigue quickly. Remember that the human eye adjusts more easily from bright light to diffuse ambient light rather than dark surroundings. Therefore, it's best to surround yourself with ambient lighting, particularly lighting that does not cause glare. Uplighting is highly recommended for areas with computers because it incurs no risk of reflection obscuring the visibility of the screen.

above
A lava lamp brings a bit of delight to the otherwise serious hard working space, which is adequately illuminated by a task lamp with a flexible arm and general overhead ambient light.

right
Balance task with the general lighting to create a comfortable work area. Place your computer screen slightly askew to windows and artificial light to prevent unwanted glare and make use of window treatments to control natural light levels.

THE BATHROOM Lighting in the bathroom is both practical and pampering—practical in that significant hygienic activities take place there every day, and pampering when the lights are turned low and the bath becomes a place of comfort and refuge. Plus, with its inevitably shiny surfaces, this room may need well-planned general illumination to soften the hard edges.

The light around the sink and mirror needs to be bright and crisp for shaving, washing, and applying makeup. It must illuminate the front and sides of the face, and shine onto the face, not into the mirror.

Thin tubes of fluorescent light, either frosted or hidden behind a louvered baffle, or a line-up of frosted incandescent bulbs placed alongside the mirror can be the answer. However, overly bright lights may be too harsh. Recessed lighting in the ceiling may be another option and offer a flattering reflection, if it is properly positioned. A light placed directly above a mirrored cabinet can sometimes throw shadows over the surface beneath it. Often lighting in this area can be more effective when it is concealed behind a protruding mirror and bounced off the ceiling, counters and walls, or used in tandem with strip lights or bulbs on the sides of the mirror.

right
Sunlight filters in and bounces off the highly reflective surfaces in this warm-toned bathroom.

Ways to Counteract Glare

Close work requires intense light balanced by ambient light. Glare is an unpleasant and sometimes dangerous side effect of the brightness desired to perform tasks in hardworking areas. Glare is usually caused by bright sunlight streaming through an exposed window or exposed sources of artificial light, incorrectly designed lighting fixtures, too much light from one direction, or excessive contrast between lighted and shadowed areas. To control glare, follow these tips:

- Curtain windows with sheer fabrics or blinds that either pull up or down to half-shield the glare of the natural light.

- Correctly shade bright sources of artificial light to diffuse or direct its brilliance. When using a directional lamp, always make sure the bare bulb is completely concealed since even a bit of exposure will produce an irritating glare.

- Bring light from two or more directions.

- Provide a low level of general illumination to diminish contrast in a room with strong task lighting. For close work, the working area should be no more than five times as bright as the darkest part of the room. A ratio of one to ten is never desirable.

Aside from the sink area, the bathroom lighting need not be overtly strong—just bright enough to accomplish daily tasks. Recessed downlights can create subtle pools of light that reflect off the tiled shower walls or mirrored surfaces. A dimmer switch can set the mood for that soothing bath, or allow the lights to be turned up for reading in the tub. Skylights can bring in natural light. A small light inside the cabinet, triggered when the door is opened, can be convenient for reading the labels of cosmetics and medicines. Whether a toilet is sequestered in its own cubicle or open to the rest of the room, it should also be well-lit.

Safety is an issue in the bathroom. Many fixtures are specifically designed for use in proximity to water. In general, freestanding, hanging, or adjustable light fixtures should be avoided, as should standard sockets, switches, and cords. A night light strong enough to make it possible to fill a glass of water or use the toilet should also be present for nocturnal visits to the bathroom.

above
The understated design of this bathroom is matched by its simple lighting solution.

left
Enjoy the old-fashioned bathing experience complete with an abundance of warm daylight filtering through blinded windows.

> **Types** of Light

The term lamp is usually used to refer to freestanding fixtures but, technically, a lamp is what is most commonly called a light bulb. The bulb itself is merely the outer envelope of an artificial light source, which contains a variety of gases and other elements that produce correspondingly varied light. Those components, and the way an electric current is passed through the bulb, gives the light its quality and color and qualifies it as either fluorescent or incandescent.

> Incandescent Lamps

These are simple devices that consist of a wire, called a filament, sealed in a bulb that is filled with gas. An electric current passing through the wire heats it until it incandesces, or glows. The diameter and length of the filament determine the amount of electrical current, or wattage, that is consumed by the lamp, and regulates its light output.

There are many types of incandescent lamps, all of which use tungsten wires sealed in bulbs filled with several gases. Incandescent lamps produce a yellow light that is most like the sun and accents the warm colors of the spectrum. However, the colors in a room can also look a little yellower than they really are under this kind of lamp. Most are inexpensive, but also don't last very long and start losing brightness as they age. Two types of incandescent lamps produce whiter lights and have longer lives: full-spectrum incandescents and halogen lamps.

Full-spectrum incandescent lamps emit a slightly whiter light that is closer to daylight and gives a truer, more vibrant cast to colors, which can be quite uplifting in a dreary space. But they can also make a room inside a house feel like it is outdoors. They are more expensive than regular incandescent bulbs, but last longer.

Halogen bulbs are filled with the gas halogen instead of the more common argon, nitrogen, or krypton. They produce a whiter brighter light that accents colors more accurately unless dimmed, when the light becomes warm and reddish. Halogen bulbs are smaller and more energy-efficient than other incandescent lamps, and last about three times longer. But halogen lamps have many drawbacks. They produce a small, intense light from a tiny bulb, so shadows are sharper and harsher reflections make it more difficult to see. They can also get very hot, sometimes radiating so much heat that particles of dust or dirt on them smoke; they can even cause fires. Finally, these lamps are extremely fragile, much more expensive than regular incandescent bulbs, and may be difficult to replace, depending on their size and shape.

> Fluorescent Lamps

A fluorescent lamp produces light by passing an electric current through a vapor or gas rather than through a tungsten wire. This is called a discharge source and is a much more efficient method than that used to heat filaments in incandescent lamps. Though there are several types of discharge lamps besides fluorescents, such as high-intensity discharge (HID) lamps, these are not suitable for residential or interior uses because they take quite a bit of time to warm up and emit light.

Fluorescent bulbs are much more expensive to purchase and install than incandescent bulbs, but they are also much more economical in the long run because they produce at least three times the light for an equivalent wattage, last ten times as long, and emit less heat into a room, which is advantageous in warm climates and the summer months. Their light distribution is also more even, and the intensity does not diminish with age. Fluorescent bulbs produce a cool white light whose quality is similar to natural light and is ideal for ambient illumination; this is fine by day but can be a drawback at night, as it can make a room feel bright and unnatural.

However, warmer full-spectrum fluorescents called compact fluorescent bulbs are on the mar-

Nothing shy about the light and color in this kitchen. The band of fluorescent lights set in the cabinets is supplemented by over head spots for more demure lighting levels for dining.

ket. Though they've been available for about a decade, recent improvements in the design and color resolution of these bulbs have increased their desirability for home use. Now their color-rendering properties are similar to the warm, mellow tones of incandescent light, and they come in shapes and sizes that are effective for home use. Though initially more expensive, these fluorescents save money in the long run because they last six to eight years (which makes them ideal for hard-to-reach places), use one-quarter of the energy of incandescent bulbs, and don't pose the same hazards as halogen lamps (which are a fire hazard).

Best of all, the savings are substantial when using this type of bulb. A 23-watt fluorescent bulb replaces a 75- to 90-watt incandescent and costs about $10 to $12, but it burns for 6,000 to 10,000 hours (or three years, based on eight hours a day of usage) and saves $20 in energy costs a year. Multiply that $20 by fourteen, which is two bulbs per room in a seven-room home, and you've saved $280 a year. Spread over three years, that's over $800 for an initial $8 to $12 investment.

> **Window** Coverings: Controlling Natural Light

We strive to bring natural light into our homes, but sometimes the light is too bright or the reflection too distracting. Control of natural light is particularly important in work areas, where interior light levels are highly concentrated.

Window treatments are the answer. These solve many other problems as well; they limit both summer heat gain and winter heat loss, screen for privacy or eliminate an unpleasant view, improve the window's appearance, and intro- duce color or texture into the room. Window treatments are also flexible in that they adjust to the changing natural light conditions of day and night. Here's a basic list of window treatment types:

> **Blinds or shades:** These come in several types. The generic blind or shade is a piece of cloth or heavy paper on a spring roll; it is usually pulled down from the top but can be made to open from the bottom or side.

> **Roman and Austrian blinds:** Considered traditional in design, these matchstick or slat blinds are usually thin bamboo or wood strips that pull up into a roll.

> **Venetian blinds:** These come in horizontal (most common) and vertical designs and are made of wood, plastic, or aluminum in a variety of colors and finishes. Contemporary design favors blinds with narrow slats (5/8 inches).

> **Thermal shades:** These energy-saving shades are made of plastic sheet or special weaves that provide sun controls through tiny microlouvers. Light and heat sensors can adjust thermal shades for optimal benefit.

> **Drapery:** This broad category includes any loosely hung fabric that covers an entire window and extends from floor to ceiling or wall to wall. Sheer fabrics permit some light transmission. Heavier fabrics or several layers further control light levels. Drapery introduces aesthetic considerations at window openings, offering color, pattern, and various kinds of textiles.

> **Curtains:** Curtains are a modest form of drapery in that they are usually placed within the window frame and offer limited light and vision control. Styles include sash, café, lace, and net curtains.

> **Shutters:** These moveable structures can be solid or louvered and may be used in combination with shades, curtains, and drapery.

> **Shoji screens:**
These light-transmitting screen panels slide on tracks and are based on Japanese tradition.

above
Pendants hang over the breakfast bar and cooking island and contribute to the sleek style of this breakfast nook. A narrow-slatted, pull-up blind controls the amount of natural light that enters the room.

Hanging lanterns always seem to evoke a feeling of a simple, more romantic time, especially when they're hanging from a beautiful hook. You can make one or more of these in a palette to suit any mood or room, with readily available and inexpensive materials. Any small glass with a lip for the chain to be fastened to will work well. Try using different styles of chains, painting several differently shaped glasses the same way, or painting the glasses a solid color.

Marbled Hanging Lantern

Materials

- Gallery glass paints in the following colors: clear frost, denim blue, royal blue, and turquoise
- Glass container with lip
- Jewelry chain
- Five silver-tone jumprings
- A closed loop for hanging, such as an earring jewelry finding
- Water-based acrylic craft sealer
- A soft paint brush
- A wire cutter or old scissors
- String
- Two pairs of pliers

TIP To ensure that you don't accidentally touch the areas you've already covered, try painting the lantern upside-down on a lazy susan, or set it on a piece of cardboard, which you can rotate as you paint.

1. Fit the glass with the hanging chain.

Wrap a piece of string under the lip of the glass to measure the circumference. Use this as a guide to measure and cut the chain. Then, cut the chain in half, and connect two ends with a jumpring. You can do this by using two pairs of pliers to pull apart a jumpring where it is separated, then pulling it closed once the chains are hooked through it. Secure the chain to the glass with a piece of masking tape to hold it in position, loop another jumpring to the other end of the chain, and test the fit. Then remove the chain.

2. Paint the glass container.

This paint sets quickly and becomes translucent after it dries completely. I recommend getting used to the paint and the painting technique described below first by painting a bottle or jar.

Squeeze out dime-sized amounts of paint on the surface of the glass, beginning with the clear frost, then use a toothpick to swirl the colors together until you have the desired marbled effect. Work in small sections, blending the edges of the area you've just painted with the new paint you add, and be sure to spread the paint out evenly in a thin layer. Paint back and forth, rather than circling in one direction, so that the area you painted first doesn't dry before you reach the edge of it. Once the paint begins to set, it can become lumpy if you try to marble it. The paint can be washed off easily before it dries, if you want to start over. Let the paint dry overnight, then apply two coats of sealer to protect the finish.

3. Attach the hanging chain.

Cut two equal lengths of chain. Open the jumpring that connects the collar that you've already assembled for the glass, loop it around one of the chains you've just cut, and close it off. Then, position the chain around the lip of the glass and use the tape to hold it in position. Using another jumpring, connect the ends of the lantern's collar, then loop the final chain in the jumpring and close.

Add a jumpring to the two loose ends of the chains. Use the last jumpring to connect them to the hook or loop for hanging.

Henna patterns, used to decorate the hands and feet of Indian brides, often have an appealing, highly stylized natural theme such as the flowers on this lampshade. With a permanent fabric marker, you can easily reproduce the color and delicate linework of this traditional art form. A thin but tightly woven fabric takes the marker best. You can create your own henna patterns by consulting one of the readily available sourcebooks or kits for doing your own henna body art.

Henna Pattern Lamp

Materials

- 1/4 inch (.5 cm) yard of off-white cotton fabric
- 1 package of 1/4 inch (.5 cm) double-fold bias binding, off-white
- Self-adhesive lampshade, 3 inch x 5 inch x 4 inch (8 cm x 13 cm x 10 cm)
- Marvy Uchida fabric brush marker in brown
- Fabric transfer paper
- Fabric glue
- Scissors
- Simple black lamp base that takes the smaller "candle" bulbs

TIP To easily experiment with different designs or to see how something will look, cut out a piece of paper in the shape of your shade, sketch the design on it, and tape it over the shade's protective wrapper. You can also make your own complete pattern this way.

1. Cut the fabric for the shade.

Prewash and iron all fabric. Tape the fabric to your work surface, and trace the shape of the lampshade wrapper on the fabric with a pencil. Cut the fabric along this line.

2. Draw the pattern onto the fabric.

Before beginning to draw the pattern, get used to the fabric marker on a scrap. The thickness and thinness of the lines are controlled by the amount of pressure you use, and you can produce calligraphy-like lines.

Copy the pattern to be 2 1/2 inches (6 cm) tall. Secure the paper and fabric with tape. Transfer the pattern to the fabric using fabric transfer paper, or trace over a light box; space four of the images about 1 inch (3 cm) apart from each other. Do not draw the border yet. Use the brown fabric brush marker to draw the design.

3. Attach the fabric to the shade.

Starting at the seam, wrap the shade with the fabric. Fold the other edge under, securing with a little fabric glue, then use the glue to secure the seam.

4. Add the trim.

Cut 9 inches (23 cm) of trim for the top of the shade and 18 inches (46 cm) for the bottom. Using fabric glue, secure it to the edges of the shade, inside and out.

5. Draw the border at the top and bottom.

The fabric stretches once it's attached to the shade, so it is difficult to get a border to match up. The easiest way to do this is to freehand draw it on after the fabric is attached.

Draw a line around the top and bottom of the shade about 1/8 inch (.25 cm) from the trim. Then, draw dots close to the lines all the way around, then follow with another line after the dots. Finish with little "commas" with the tails ending at the lines.

Lighting All Around the House

From the entrance to the house to the most hidden corner of the basement closet, consistent light levels are an essential ingredient—and often taken for granted. Here is one scenario: A set of decorative lanterns guides you inside your house. You flick on the recessed hall lights without concern for what might be waiting in the dark. You pass through the brightly lit hallway to the basement stairs.

As your foot hits the first step, the movement sensor trips the light switch, turning on the fluorescent ceiling light below. You hurry to the far corner of the basement without a thought about how easily you are finding your way in the once-dark cellar. You open the closet door. A small halogen bulb switches on. Deep in the closet are the tennis balls you almost forgot to take. You turn around and, as you go, the lights switch off behind you. The progression is automatic.

We need light in hallways, foyers, stairs, and basements to safely negotiate our way. The trick is to reach beyond the purely practical to the aesthetic. Meet the need for light throughout the house while making a theatrical statement or generating a warm and relaxing atmosphere. Rather than just lighting a staircase from above, position a sequence of recessed wall lights so that the light grazes each stair tread and riser to create a playful visual image. Use lighting to create a sense of progression at the entrance or to heighten the exterior architectural drama. Think of a long, narrow passageway as an opportunity for display with downlights or uplights. Use spotlights to turn a garden into a nighttime room. Light can be used to enliven the dullest spaces.

left
Add surprise and delight to a room with decorative lighting.

above

With strategically placed spots, turn your closet into a stage set.

left

Try a creative touch to lighting hallways. Place lights in the stair treads to supplement overhead lights. Glass block provides a translucent wall material that allows the transfer of natural or artificial light.

below

A highly stylized crystal and wrought-iron lantern sets the stage for the home's interior design.

LIGHTING SPECIAL-NEEDS AREAS (HALLWAYS, FOYERS, STAIRS, BASEMENTS) When we think about lighting our home, we overlook some spaces that get the most use—the hallways, foyers, and stairs. And not only do we forget how critical adequate illumination can be in these spaces, we tend to think of them as areas where function takes precedence over form. In fact, both count in the case of the hallway and foyer, and it is so easy to use lighting as a decorative tool, why not try to make the basement as attractive and charming as possible?

The foyer is the space guests see first. A half- or indistinctly lit foyer makes it harder to engage the warm note of hospitality than one gently illuminated with ambient ceiling or wall lights. If the space is used to display photographs, artwork, or collectibles, consider spotlights or track lighting. Use recessed downlights or directed spots to accentuate the path from the front door to the rest of the home. Create a sense of drama and architectural distinction with wall-mounted uplights. Any of these techniques, alone or in combination, allow you to welcome your guests and make it easy for them to admire your home.

The hallway need not have the most pedestrian style in the home. An antique ceiling light can add a decorative flourish, as can pendant lights, if the ceiling is high and the lights are not hung too low. Sconces that protrude from the wall on arms or branches reflect on painted woodwork and polished floors. Recessed downlights mark the path, as do wall-mounted sconces or uplights. If the hall is wide enough, a lamp on a small shelf or table in a corner is a pleasant touch. If possible, add skylights to the hall's ceiling to bring in natural light during the day, or lighten the hallway with a strategically placed mirror that will expand the space and reflect illumination.

The most common way to light the stairway is with ceiling lights at the top and bottom. Avoid that old-fashioned approach by installing wall-mounted or recessed lights along the treads at foot or shoulder level. Lights at foot level work best for safety reasons; shoulder-level lights are for aesthetic effect. Be careful with angle or pendant lighting, which can cause glare. A skylight at the top of the staircase can add a dramatic natural effect.

above

During the day, natural light filters into the hallway through the glass block wall inserts. At night, the hallway is illuminated by uplights placed in the floor.

right

Bookshelves offer an unexpected lighting source. Place tube lights underneath each shelf to brighten up a cove or a dark hallway.

Basements often serve many purposes—storage area, laundry, playroom, workshop, music room. The new shapes, sizes, and color renditions of fluorescent lights find utilitarian use in basements, where the value of long-lasting light outweighs the desire for pure aesthetics. Ceiling or wall-mounted lights work best in places of high activity. Incandescent lighting should also be considered in the basement, since it can bring softness to a hardworking space.

above
Increase safety and beauty by lighting stair treads. Simply place sidelights in the walls next to the stairs.

left
Brighten stairs by inserting sidelights at tread level.

LIGHTING OUTDOOR AREAS Outdoor areas are lit for security, but also for safety and beauty. The larger the house and the more isolated the location, the more lights are generally required. In urban areas, street lighting can provide some visual aid, but probably not enough to allow you to get the key in the lock on a dark night or appropriately welcome visitors. However, overlighting can also be a problem, since it can cause illumination or glare to spill over into the windows of nearby houses.

Effective exterior lighting doesn't necessarily have to be bright. Spotlights can be used to illuminate the pathway to the house, along either the driveway or the front walkway. Carriage lamps or lanterns at the front door warmly beckon to the visitor. Position the lights carefully to avoid glare. A grand building façade may be lit with several spotlights focused on the most impressive architectural details or contrasts in textures or patterns. Flooding the façade dulls the building's appearance. Locate lights at low positions and create pools of light.

_right
Selectively placed hanging lanterns and table lamps create a room outdoors and extend your living space.

Gardens offer a delightful stage for lighting. Back light foliage, silhouette garden structures, spot light ornamental pots, all for theatrical play and variety of scale and proportion. Ornamental lighting can be provided through uplights inserted in the ground or lanterns set on the ground, or even downlights. Use higher lighting levels in the barbecue area—or at least provide for stronger lighting when food is being prepared.

For safety reasons, consult a qualified professional when planning outdoor lighting installations. Outdoor lighting needs its own infrastructure, and should be installed by a professional. Fixtures and wires are constantly exposed to weather, extremes of temperature, and lawnmowers and garden tools, and must be safe and sturdy. Switches should be operable from indoors.

_**above**
Colorful lanterns define an outdoor room.

_**left**
Exterior lighting should spot distinctive features of your house, as well as provide paths of access and a warm welcome.

> **Turning** a Garden into an **Outdoor** Room

Indoor-outdoor living is popular, especially among people who live in a small house or a mild climate. Lit creatively, a garden patio can be a glorious extension of the home, offering the grandest nighttime entertainment spot. A lighting scheme that creates a certain mood makes or breaks the space. Bright floodlighting won't produce the intimacy desired. Rather, think of the pools of light that you try to create indoors. Here are some suggestions:

> **Concentrate** on soft, glowing light levels.

> **Start** with candles, torches, and lanterns.

> **Use** uplights and accents around the patio directed toward the surrounding plantings to dramatize the different shapes and textures of the plants.

> **Use** small spotlights, like string lights used for Christmas trees, to highlight an area where food is served or embellish particularly attractive trees.

> **Section** off parts of the yard with borders made of votives, but position them so they won't be easy to knock over.

> **Create** more than one focal point for your outdoor room to express the pools-of-light idea.

> **Consider** how to build the light from dusk-to-dark night in your outdoor room to create a sense of heightening drama. You can do this by turning the lights on in various areas in stages.

> **Build** flexibility into your outdoor room so that it can be lit differently from time to time.

> **Create** a structural presence in your room with a trellis or arch, which can be imaginatively lit from below.

> **Line** pathways with votives on the ground, placed out of the way of feet, or string lights draped along low bushes or trees.

Safety First

Safety is a double-edged sword when it comes to lighting. We need light to make our way safely around the house, yet at the same time, we need to be aware of the safety issues surrounding light and electricity. Here many ways to cope with potential hazards:

- Light stairs, halls, and passageways well, so you can get safely around your house.

- Avoid overly bright lighting that can cause glare and deep shadows. Light all stairwells. Illuminate exterior entrances adequately for security purposes. Use timers to operate lights when away from home.

- Don't guess at electrical installations; consult a professional for indoor and outdoor wiring.

- Make sure you provide enough ventilation room with recessed lighting. The hotter the bulb, the more ventilation it needs.

- Make sure water and electricity do not come in contact in bathrooms and kitchens.

- Watch for faulty wiring or plugs and overloaded sockets.

- Light bulbs get hot, especially halogen lamps. For instance, the heat from a 300-watt halogen bulb can top 900 °F and scorch surfaces 18 inches away, so don't place these lamps near surfaces they can damage.

- Don't place lamps near drapes, curtains, or wall hangings that could billow in a breeze and brush against them or tip the lamps over and be ignited from the heat.

- Don't' leave hot bulbs on for long periods in room unattended, as they can be a fire hazard if they shatter, tip over, or scorch something nearby that ignites.

- Don't leave anything draped over a lamp arm or lampshade (either accidentally or purposely, such as a piece of cloth to change the lamp's mood), as it can catch fire from the heat of the bulb.

- Don't look directly at a powerful lamp. The intense glare and heat, especially from halogen lamps, can harm your eyes.

> **All** About Bulbs

Bulbs are often referred to as lamps, which is the technically correct term for the glass that encases a filament or holds some type of gas and glows when electricity is applied.

Information on the shape and size of each lamp or bulb is imprinted on it. Shape is identified by a letter, while size relates to the bulb's diameter at its widest point and is identified in 1/8-inch multiples. For instance, an A-21 bulb has an A (standard) shape and a 21-inch by 1/8-inch (or 2 5/8-inch) diameter.

Make sure you know the shape and size of the bulb that is needed before going to the store. When shopping for a new fixture, it pays to take bulb shape and size into consideration, as some bulbs are hard to find or must be custom ordered. This is particularly important with imported fixtures. Finally, when buying a fixture for a hard-to-reach spot, consider one that can use the new long-life compact fluorescent bulbs, which need not be replaced very often. When possible, install dimmers, as

reducing the level of light by as little as 10 percent can increase the life of a bulb and sometimes even double it and provide more lighting level options.

The most common type of incandescent lamps is the standard frosted or opaque GLS (general lighting service) bulb. Silvered-bowl GLS bulbs, the simplest type of incandescent reflectors, throw light back into specially designed fixtures or are used to prevent glare in pendant fixtures. Opal white globe bulbs are also quite common and emit a soft, diffused light that doesn't cast hard shadows. Candle-shaped bulbs, which emulate the glow of candlelight, come in several slender shapes that are frosted or clear, depending on whether or not they are to be used with shades (the frosted variety is intended to be used without

shades). Parabolic aluminized reflector (PAR) economy bulbs have a sturdy front made of thick, textured glass that enables them to withstand higher temperatures and are available as incandescent or halogen lamps. Reflectors come in two versions: a spot that emits a beam of light less than 30-degrees wide, and a flood that emits a beam of light greater than 30-degrees wide.

Halogen lamps burn at much higher temperatures than regular incandescent lamps, so the bulb is smaller and made of quartz to withstand the higher heat. Standard household-current halogen bulbs are used in conventional fixtures; tiny, compact low-voltage halogen bulbs require transformers to reduce the power. Low-voltage halogen diachronic reflector bulbs, which must also be used with transformers, direct light forward and draw heat back, which creates a concentrated beam of cool light.

Fluorescent lamps have been traditionally used in commercial applications, thanks to the cool white nature of the light they emit, but they are now available in compact sizes that have warm color-rendering properties closer to that of incandescents. They cost more in the short run but last six to eight years, use approximately one-quarter the energy of regular incandescent bulbs, and come in a wide range of shapes. Now there are fluorescent bulbs that emulate the standard form of the familiar GLS incandescent bulb and tread new ground with their innovative designs that sport coiled, slim, and circular shapes. Even so, they fit a variety of standard fixtures and provide cheaper, brighter, and more efficient light. While there are no hard-and-fast rules when it comes to choosing a type of bulb, some helpful guidelines are available:

> **As a general rule,** the lamp in a fitting should be shielded from view because it can be extremely irritating, distracting, and harsh on the eye. Overly bright, badly positioned bulbs can actually cause temporary blinding.

> **Certain light bulbs** have a specific decorative purpose. Flame-tipped bulbs, which are also called candelabra bulbs, simulate candles, and, if frosted, can remain exposed in sconces. Tinted bulbs can be used to give a warm glow to a room, cool down its colors, or dress it up for a special occasion. While incandescent bulbs come in a variety of tints, fluorescents can be covered with colored sleeves or manipulated with sheets of cellophane gel (which are clipped over the opening in a shade to tint the emitted light). Both of these products are routinely sold at lighting or photographic supply stores.

> **Reflector bulbs come** in floodlights and spotlights, and have a reflective silver coating inside the glass to direct light forward and provide better beam control than general service bulbs. When compared with a general purpose bulb of the same wattage, this treatment can double the amount of light (in foot-candles) thrown on a subject or spot.

> **Handling a bulb** shortens its life because dirt, grease, or moisture from fingers can cause it to shatter once it is turned on (halogen bulbs are particularly susceptible to this). Use a cloth or paper towel when installing bulbs, first making sure the fixture is turned off at the power source

High-Tech Lighting Accessories

We're all familiar with the automatic switch that turns on the refrigerator light when the door is open and off when the door is closed. These switches also work well in hall closets and other storage areas. To give the impression of occupancy, install timers and time switches on lights in the kitchen and other heavily used rooms. More advanced are approach lights that can be triggered by heat, motion, or sound. Some switches are tripped by infrared beams, which are good security devices. It is likely that the fully computerized home of the future will be equipped with photosensitive cells that switch lights on and off in response to natural light levels or the approach of a potential user. Or the lighting of the whole home may be programmed to turn on or off at certain times. The goal is a more efficient and economical use of energy. Some of this technology is already in use in theaters and large commercial and public spaces.

>**All** About Lamps and Shades

Like the right piece of jewelry or scarf, a lamp can make a major impact on the style quotient of a room. Plus, an astonishing range of interesting and innovative lamps is on the market today, ranging from intricate antiques or reproduction versions to cleverly conceived contemporary designs that employ materials in new ways and boast sleek or sculptural lines. In fact, some of these are functional works of art in their own right (see Decorative Lamps Tip.)

above
Custom-made, decorative table lamps come in all sizes and shapes and are as individual as the craftsmen themselves.

Lamps can also be made easily from a wide range of objects, such as vases, jars, and coffee- or tea-pots, thanks to simple, do-it-yourself adapter kits readily available at craft, hardware, and lighting stores. Almost any object can work as a base, as long as it is stable, hollow, and has center holes through both ends (but don't drill holes in an antique, as this destroys its value).

The shade is an often overlooked but critical component of a lamp. Shades that are dark in hue glow softly when a light is turned on, those made of translucent materials cast more light into a room and make a space seem brighter, and opaque shades direct the light rather than emit it. But all shades dictate where light falls by their shapes. Those with a wider diameter cast a larger pool of light than narrower shades, though repositioning a shade with respect to the bulb changes this equation, as the closer the bulb to the bottom edge of the shade, the larger the pool of light.

Besides regulating the way light is dispersed, shades can make or break the lamp aesthetically. Take the lamp base to the store and try it out with various shades before making any decisions—especially if the lamp is an important accessory in a room. Though one formu-

la dictates that the diameter of the bottom of the shade should be equal to the height of the base, this approach is unreliable. The ultimate success of the marriage of base and shade depends on the shape, style, color, and composition of both parts of the lamp. When choosing shades, keep the following points in mind:

> **Consider function first.** If a lamp is intended for task lighting, use an opaque shade that directs light down; if it is intended for general lighting, use a translucent shade that casts a broad and soft glow. Shape also affects how light is dispersed. The three main shade shapes are drum, which is cylindrical; empire, which is slightly wider at the bottom; and coolie, which resembles the hats worn by Chinese peasants and has broadly sloping sides.

> **Pick a style that suits the decor of the room.** Checkerboards and stenciled motifs evoke a rustic or country demeanor, muted florals or simple laces can be unabashedly romantic, pleated or plain silks can be elegant and formal, and textured or grainy papers can be contemporary and sophisticated.

above

Choose a lamp that expresses the decorative mood of a room or a painting near by.

> **Pick the right size.**
Relate the shade to the scale of the base first, the scale of any surrounding furnishings next, and the scale of the room last. The visual weight of the lamp base, not its actual dimensions, should be about two-thirds the entire lamp, with the shade making up the remaining third. Between the shade's bottom edge and the surface it rests on, the distance should be greater than the shade height so the lamp doesn't look top-heavy. The shade should also extend at least two inches beyond the base on all sides.

> **Check the positioning of the shade on the lamp base.**
Shades feature one of two types of carriers: a metal structure that attaches to the base, or a metal structure that hugs the bulb. In both cases, the shade should hide all of the metal working parts of the base when viewed from eye level.

> **View the shade with the bulb illuminated.**
The color, material, and shape of the shade have a profound effect on the quality of light the lamp emits, so make sure the shade fulfills your wants and needs before purchasing it.

above and right
Like a giant sea anemone, the brilliant object nestled in the corner seems to have a life of its own. You wonder, if you turn your head, if it will slink into a different position.

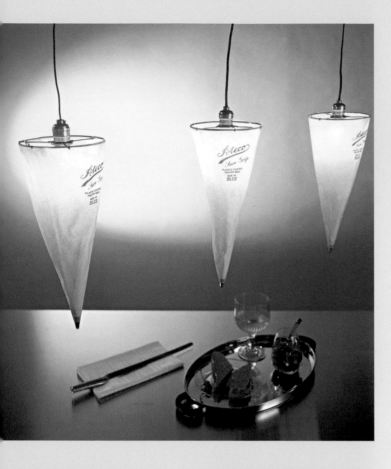

Decorative Lamps:
Style over Substance

Consumers are asking a lot of lighting designers these days. Not only do we want functional lights, we desire aesthetically pleasing lamps. And manufacturers are responding with everything from high-tech floor lamps to antique replica chandeliers. Purely decorative lamps, however, go a step further. These lamps display light as an art object and are quirky, fun, playful. Often the lamps are not bright enough to read or do hard tasks by, but they are wonderful to look at and magical to have in one's home.

■ Perhaps the easiest way to envision a decorative lamp is in the children's world. There are carousel lamps that project cartoon images of favorite characters, animals, stars, or plants onto the walls; ceramic figures or colorful paper shapes that light up; and lamp bases made of actual toys or pieces of sports equipment, ranging from baseball bats to dolls.

■ Decorative lamps for adults are much more abstract, relying on the pure imagination of the artist. The light can move, like the flickering of a candle, or shine intensely, like neon gas. It can sparkle behind a sculpture representing a leaf or an abstract globe. Tiny lamps can produce jewel-like sparkles.

■ Decorative lamps are sometimes available at lamp stores, mixed in with more conventional lighting. They are more likely to be found at arts and crafts shows, art galleries, and artist studios. Decorative lamps can add an unusual element of delight and artistry to your home.

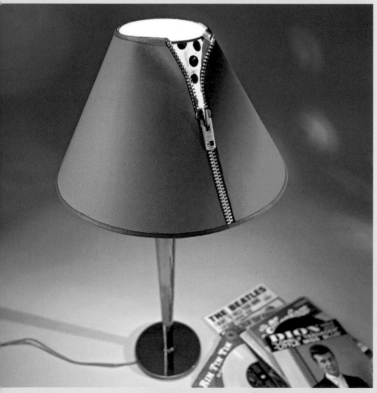

left

Two contemporary versions of the decorative lamp.

above

Consider light as sculpture. Light can have an artistic purpose as well as a utilitarian one, as seen in this playful bedroom wall hanging, which supports the popular "points of light" metaphor.

A simple shell can shed a warm, soothing light and soften the look of a utilitarian night light, and the easily added pearlescent foiling adds a natural-looking shimmery effect. When selecting a shell, test it against a bulb to be sure it is translucent enough. Rather then using a single shell, you could try gluing small, thin shells together in a fan shape.

Pearled Shell Night Light

Materials
- Standard night-light, with removable front
- Shell
- Delta Renaissance Foil in mother-of-pearl
- Delta Renaissance Foil adhesive
- Delta Renaissance Foil sealer
- Soft brush
- Hot glue gun or strong general-purpose adhesive

TIP Beautiful shells that are large enough to serve as a night light shade may be difficult to find. I used a simple scallop shell, which diffuses light beautifully, and are often sold at kitchen supply stores as seafood serving dishes.

1. Apply the adhesive to the shell.
Select a shell that is fairly flat and has an area at the bottom that can be fitted to the night light.

Following the manufacturer's instructions, apply a thick even coat of adhesive to the shell using a soft brush. Try not to go over the same area twice, as this may result in the adhesive becoming textured or lumpy. When the adhesive has dried and become translucent, apply a second coat and let it dry until it has become translucent.

2. Apply foil.
Cut a piece of foil big enough to cover the shell, plus a little extra to leave unattached for easier removal. Lay the foil on the shell and smooth it out gently with your fingers. Using sharp objects will damage the foil, so use something soft for crevices, such as cotton swab or eraser. The shell I used had many grooves and a lot of texture, so I had to go over the shell several times, concentrating on small areas each time. Try not to touch the bare adhesive with your fingers, and be sure not to let the exposed foil backing touch the adhesive, as it will pull it off.

3. Seal the shell.
The foiled shell is prone to scratches and fingerprints, so carefully apply one or two coats of sealer to protect it before attaching it to the night light.

4. Attach the shell to night light.
Fit the shell to the night light to see where the two meet, and put two or three small dabs of hot glue on the shell at this point. Press it to the night light, trying not to let the glue be visible from the front. Add a few more dabs of glue inside, if necessary, and hold the shell in position until the glue firms up, about one minute. If you need to, remove the shell before the hot glue has dried and try again; it should be easily removable at this point.

Hot glue is ideal because of the quick bond and easy removal, but you can use a strong, industrial adhesive. Be sure it is formulated for a variety of surfaces, including plastic.

Two or three of these tea lights can be used for an intimate table setting, or en masse for a festive effect. With a simple foiling system, you can make these in copper, gold, or silver. Try "painting" a simple pattern with the adhesive, such as stripes, rather than foiling the whole votive, or unifying differently shaped votives with the same pattern.

Silvered Tea Light Votives

Materials
- Small glass votives
- Delta Renaissance Foil in silver
- Delta Renaissance Foil adhesive
- Delta Renaissance Foil sealer
- Soft brush

TIP To get the best effect from the semi-opaque foiling, use smaller glass containers such as those used for tea lights, so the flame will be closer to the glass.

1. Apply the adhesive.
Clean and dry the votives. Following the manufacturer's instructions, apply a thick even coat of adhesive to the votives using a soft brush. Try not to go over the same area twice, as this may result in the adhesive becoming textured or lumpy. When the adhesive has dried and become translucent, apply a second coat and let it dry until it has become translucent.

2. Apply the foil.
Cut a piece of foil about 4 inches (10 cm) square, or large enough to cover one side of the votive. Lay the foil on the votive, being sure to leave a small section unattached for easier removal, and smooth it out gently with your fingers. Using sharp objects will damage the foil, so use something soft for crevices, such as cotton swab or eraser. Repeat until the votive is covered. Go over bare spots with more foil, but be sure not to let the exposed foil backing touch the adhesive, as it will pull it off.

3. Seal the votives.
The foiled votives are prone to scratches and fingerprints, so carefully apply one or two coats of sealer to protect them.

Addressing Special Lighting Needs/
Lighting Solutions

The subject of lighting can be needlessly complex. While focusing on technical advice about fixtures and bulbs, we forget to rely on our most reliable tool for assessing lighting effectiveness—our own eyes. It is easy to distinguish between good and bad lighting, or adequate and inadequate lighting, merely by looking at it. When you live in a room and perform a range of activities or tasks there daily, its faults become all too apparent.

Good lighting meets your needs, puts you at ease, creates a sense of comfort, blends into the background, and enhances the colors, forms, and textures of the furnishings in a room. Bad lighting is jarring and leaves you with the impression that something is amiss. It may imbue a space with an uneasy atmosphere or make its occupants jumpy, nervous, and tense. More significantly, it can cause headaches, eyestrain, nervousness, or even accidents due to poor visibility.

left
In an exceedingly narrow room with high ceilings, the headboard was placed on the side of the bed and flanked by wall mounted reading lamps that swivel to different positions.

In the end, the specific purpose and design of a room as well as the wants, needs, and personalities of its users determine the look, intensity, and distribution of its lighting. Fortunately, there are plenty of ways to improve the caliber, quality, and ambience of the lighting in a room without incurring the mess and upheaval of running wires into ceilings and walls. It is possible to change the mood of a room, up its style or drama quotient, or improve its performance with a few simple changes or tricks. Here are some of the simple principles the pros apply in using lighting as a tool throughout the home.

above
Dress up the traditional light shade.

right, above
Eclectic lamps complement the room's creative décor.

right, below
A whimsical interpretation of bedside reading lamps.

LIGHT AND COLOR Artificial lighting can do unexpected things to the colors of furnishings and textiles. Incandescent lamps, which emit most of their light at the yellow to red end of the spectrum, add yellow to everything they illuminate. Accordingly, blue assumes a greenish cast, red an orange cast, and white a creamy cast. Halogen bulbs, which are also incandescent, produce a whiter light, but when set on a dimmer at low, they assume a reddish glow. Fluorescent light is a cool, bright white light that can be annoyingly sterile and white, but the new compact fluorescent bulbs cast a warmer glow that is quite close to the tones of incandescent lamps. To avoid a room that works only at day or night, check the color of upholstery, rugs, drapes, and paint under all the lighting conditions of a twenty-four-hour period. Paint a piece of wallboard or plywood (several feet square) the same color you plan on painting the walls; check it at all times of the day and night to see how the light affects it.

above
With five willowy arms, this floor lamp is able to fulfill many lighting needs at one time.

left
A discrete multiple-spot provides diffuse ambient lighting in this sitting room that by day is flooded with natural light.

INCREASING LIGHT BY DAY Dark walls and surfaces, especially those with matte finishes, absorb light. This applies to everything in a room, including walls, window treatments, upholstered pieces, and rugs. At its most basic, increasing the light in a room involves using light colors on surfaces and furnishings. On walls, use gloss or semi-gloss paint; on furnishings, use textiles that have reflective properties, such as satin-finished fabrics and twills rather than nubby or textured textiles. To increase the light that filters into a room, use translucent rather than opaque window treatments. If a space does not get enough light from its windows, steal light from a brighter adjacent room by installing transom or fanlight windows over doors or turning complete walls into three-quarter-height partitions. It is also possible to add skylights or clerestory windows to a room. For rooms facing north, artificial light is necessary during the day. To make its presence less obvious, stick to sources that are close to natural daylight, which is whiter than incandescent light. Full-spectrum bulbs are one option; fluorescent striplighting is another. The latter can work well by day, concealed behind cornices, in the top of a bookcase, or recessed inside soffits above windows.

above
Uplights hidden behind the white bench reflect off the marble wall and compete with the natural light entering at the top of the spiral staircase.

right
The translucent shoji screen wall allows light to enter from the adjoining room, which can be supplemented by task lighting or candlelight.

INCREASING LIGHT AT NIGHT When determining how much light to use at night, the first consideration is whether the illumination should have a strong physical presence or be more of a background aura. For lots of bright light, use downlights in tracks, recessed cans, or pendant fixtures, supplemented with floor and table lamps throughout the room. To make lighting the focal point of the room, use dramatic or sculptural fixtures that emit plenty of light, and place them at even intervals around a room. Examples of this type of setup include supplementing a spectacular pendant lamp or chandelier in a dining area with interesting sconces and using wall-mounted fixtures or wall washers on the perimeter of a living room and complementing them with torchieres that reflect light off the ceiling.

A lighting plan geared for plenty of bright light can quickly be transformed into one that also provides indirect or moody illumination with the addition of dimmer switches on all of the lighting sources in the room. For even more subtlety, forego the use of floor or table lamps. For out-and-out mystery, use hidden lighting sources to provide a soft blanket of background lighting in the room. These can be recessed in the ceiling or soffits or concealed behind beams, over or under shelving and cabinets, or behind large architectural elements that can be specially designed to accommodate them, such as cornices, moldings, baseboards, and coves.

left
Utilitarian light fixtures can provide great flexibility in meeting your lighting needs and at the same time complement your aesthetic tastes.

CHANGING SPACE WITH LIGHT Lighting can have a major impact on the depth and scale of a space. To make a room feel smaller, use downlights as the primary lighting source in a room and avoid lighting the perimeter of the space by positioning lighting toward the center of the room. This draws the eye into the room rather than out to its boundaries. To implement this, hang low pendant fixtures on the ceiling and make strategic use of lamps on tables and the floor.

To lower a high ceiling, keep light away from it by placing wall lights fairly low and using shades or pendant fixtures with closed tops that won't throw any light back on the ceiling. Also, draw attention to items placed at a low level, such as pictures or hangings positioned low on the wall or groups of accessories placed on low surfaces, by lighting them from above.

To make a room feel more open, airy, and spacious than it is, use indirect reflective light to create the illusion of height and depth. Wall washers trick your eye into seeing stretches rather than sharply delineating the boundaries of walls, while uplights aimed at the tops of walls visually increase their height.

above
The glorification of the lowly light bulb into a magnificent chandelier.

right
Floor lanterns mark the way or become a piece of floor sculpture.

below
Lights set in the pedestal turn a utilitarian sink into a glassy piece of sculpture.

To make only the ceiling look higher, use floor or wall-mounted uplights to throw light up on the ceiling, or conceal lighting behind a cornice or coving mounted high on the walls at the perimeter of the room. To make a long, narrow space seem wider, focus attention on a feature at one of the end walls, such as a window with an elegant treatment or an interesting piece of art, by highlighting it with a spotlight, and wash the other walls in the room with an even but less intense light. To make a space seem larger, wash opposite walls with light to make them seem farther apart. Alternatively, combine lighting with mirrors and reflective surfaces to add the illusion of space to a room.

right

The lighting designer must create pools of artificial light to balance the natural sunlight flowing into the room.

CREATING MOODS WITH LIGHT There are myriad ways to use lighting to change the mood of a room. Some techniques focus on the color of the light, others address the decorative aspects of the fixtures, and others blend these approaches. In general, incandescent light makes a space feel warm, mellow, and cozy, thanks to the yellow tones it emits, while halogen and compact fluorescent lamps emit a cooler, whiter light that conveys a crisp, minimal, and modern aesthetic.

Fixtures in highly decorative shapes and styles lend a room their demeanor. For instance, for a rustic touch, use sconces, fixtures, lamps, even a chandelier made of a rugged material, such as wrought iron or wooden branches and boughs. For a romantic aura, choose antique or vintage fixtures, lamps, and sconces with delicate or curvy forms, and top them with pretty patterned or lacy shades. To imbue a room with a modernist or contemporary mood, choose lighting sources that are sleek and minimal, or consider concealing them with soffits, recessing them in ceilings, camouflaging them with architectural elements, or hiding them behind decorative elements such as pillars, pedestals, screens, and large plants or trees.

To make a space more intimate, use lots of table lamps to create a cozy glow and outfit them with shades in colors that are warm rather than cool, such as alabaster, pearl, parchment, or ivory instead of white, so the light they cast has a mellow tone.

left
Consider a plethora of lighting options in your main living area.

>Quick Fixes

Sometimes, changing a simple element
in a room—such as the color of the walls or
the strength of the bulbs in the fixtures and
lamps-totally changes the nature and efficacy of
its lighting. Here are quick and easy ways to correct common
illumination problems:

> **Manipulate the amount**
of light in a room with window
treatments. Translucent drapes,
curtains, and shades, which filter
natural light and produce a diffused effect, come in many
weights and should be chosen
with regard to this property.
Slatted blinds offer optimum control because they can block out all
illumination in the room, flood it
with light, or be used to strike a
balance between these extremes.

> **If there are** several light
sources in a room and the overall
effect is still unsatisfactory, change
the bulbs, which may be too bright
or too dim for their surroundings. If
a fixture or lamp emits too much
glare, reduce it by replacing a standard bulb with a reflector bulb.

> **Change the shades** in a
fixture to transform the magni-
tude and quality of the light it
emits. Translucent materials allow
more light into a room, which
makes it seem brighter. White
shades make light seem cool and
clean, while shades with creamy
hues emit more mellow tones.
Darker shades can glow softly
when the light is turned on and
lend a space drama.

> **Use colored bulbs** to
change the nature of the illumination in a space. Incandescent bulbs
come in a variety of tints, and fluorescents can be covered with colored sleeves or manipulated with
sheets of cellophane gel (which are
clipped over the opening in a
shade to tint the emitted light).

> **To make a** dark room much lighter, paint one or all of the walls a light color in a gloss or semi-gloss finish. Aim an accent light at one or two walls to reflect onto the other walls and brighten the room.

> **In a dark** corner, use a fixture with an opening at both top and bottom for more general illumination in the space. Make the corner a focal point by filling it with a tall plant or tree and positioning an uplight in front of or behind it. Experiment to find the most attractive placement.

> **If a room** is lit by a central pendant fixture that is inadequate, replace it with spotlights on a track system that runs through the central axis, or even criss-crosses it, for greater flexibility.

> **If the accent** lighting in a room isn't working, make it brighter. Accent lighting should be at least three times brighter than the general lighting in a room to highlight its intended target.

> **To instantly update** track lighting, outfit it with new fixtures or vary the fixtures on the track; they don't have to be the same and it can be both interesting and effective to mix spotlights and floodlights to create varying pools and points of light.

>**Minimum** Lighting Levels

While there are no hard-and-fast rules on how much light a specific space or room in a house needs, guidelines do exist. Keep in mind that many factors influence these suggestions, such as individual preference, the way a space is used, and the age of the individuals using the space.

While most people think of brightness in terms of wattage, professional lighting designers work in technical quantifiers such as lumens, foot-candles, and candela, using mathematical equations that are highly technical and site specific, which make them useless for the layperson. As a general rule, a room needs an average of 200 watts for every 50 square feet (4.5 square meters), and bulbs with higher lumens are more efficient given the same wattage (both lumens and wattage are listed on the package). Elderly people may need double the wattage because the pupil of the aging eye has less flexibility and eventually gets fixed in an open position that permanently demands more brightness. Average people in their fifties get as much light out of a 100-watt bulb as people in their twenties get from a 50-watt bulb.

To increase lighting in a room, either double the number of light sources or double the wattage of the bulbs, which is a more energy-efficient option if the fixtures can take it. However, keep in mind that wattage is only the beginning; the light a 100-watt bulb emits is affected by the efficiency of the fixture, the type of shade or covering over it, and its location in relation to where the light is needed.

Here are general guidelines for areas throughout the home:

> **Entry halls:** For an average 50- to 75-square-foot (4.5- to 6.75-square meter) space, use one 100-watt hanging fixture or 15-watt floodlamp in a recessed fixture.

> **Passageways:** Use one 75-watt fixture or one 100-watt recessed fixture for every 10 feet (3 meters) of hallway.

> **Closets:** For an average-sized closet, use one 100-watt fixture; for a walk-in closet, use one 100-watt recessed fixture every 10 feet (3 meters).

> **Living rooms:** Chandeliers or hanging pendants should have a low wattage and be used for decorative purposes. At a minimum, a small living room should have four table lamps or a combination of table and floor lamps. About 200 watts are needed on each wall so that a good base of background light, without harsh contrasts or deep shadows between background and task lighting, is created in the room. If a lamp is used to light an entire corner, it should carry at least 200 watts.

> **Dining rooms:** Chandeliers or hanging pendants are more important in dining rooms than in living rooms because they form a dramatic focal point over tables, but central fixtures that are too bright cause glare and visual discomfort and should be equipped with dimmers. Use low-wattage downlights (preferably recessed) on either side of a central hanging fixture for a low level of general illumination. Consider candles on the table for dramatic mood lighting. Candles should be high so diners do not look directly into the flames.

> **Bedrooms:** If a central lighting fixture is used for general illumination, it should be glare-proof (such as a shallow, frosted glass orb or disk) and about 200 watts. For reading in bed, use a table lamp no more than 25 inches (635 millimeters) away from the book or a swinging-arm wall lamp attached 12 inches (304,8 millimeters) from the bed, in line with the shoulder of the reader. Either should provide at least 100 watts of illumination, preferable on a three-way switch.

> **Dens, studies, and family rooms:** These rooms vary widely in size today, and it is necessary to approach large great rooms as a living room to obtain the correct amount of general background illumination. Table lamps and downlights are necessary to ensure enough lighting for activities such as reading, writing, playing games, and working on crafts and tasks. Three hundred watts is necessary for sewing, embroidering, or other highly detailed tasks. Downlights are also suitable for illuminating specific activity areas in the room; they should provide 250 to 300

watts to adequately light a whole area, such as a bar or game table.

> **Kitchens:** Ceiling fixtures provide a good overall level of shadowless illumination. These can be recessed or on tracks, but they should afford illumination to every single square foot of this space. Wattage needs vary according to the colors of the walls, tiles, and surface treatments in the room and the reflecting value of porcelain, tile, and metal surfaces. Avoid dark colors on countertops, as they absorb too much light, which can make certain tasks dangerous. Strip fluorescent lighting mounted under cabinets provides excellent illumination for the work surfaces below. To prevent shadows on the range and sink while working at these stations, make sure adequate

lighting sources of about 200 watts are installed directly above them.

> **Washrooms and bathrooms:** High-wattage lighting is mandatory near the mirror behind the sink, but the specific level depends on the nature of the space. For instance, when two sinks are installed in a long counter, the length of the counter dictates the brightness of the lighting, which should be above or surrounding the mirrors behind the sink (or sinks). If the room has a freestanding sink topped with a medicine cabinet, use sconces or bracketed fixtures of at least 100 watts each on either side of the mirrored cabinet.

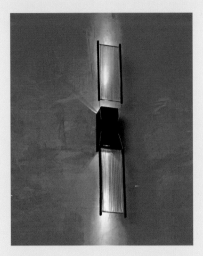

above
Glass wings reflect the sconce's light vertically.

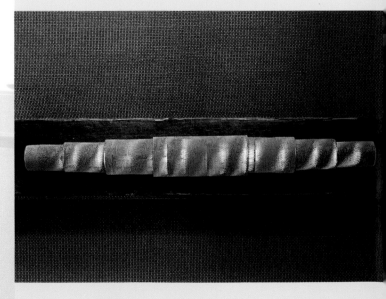

above
Available in various shapes, sizes, and textures, a decorative sconce can set the mood for a hallway or room.

A delightfully whimsical showcase for the light bulb—and the milk bottle.

>**Glossary:**
In the Know

Technical terms can be confusing. Here's what you need to know:

Accent lighting is interchangeable with decorative lighting and refers to the illumination directed at a specific object or area of a space to draw attention to it. It is used to enhance certain features or furnishings in a space, such as architectural elements, shelves, armoires, collections of objects, decorative accessories, or art.

Ambient lighting is interchangeable with background or general lighting, and refers to the indirect illumination that fills the volume of a room and creates a general foundation of adequate lighting for all the activities in a room or space.

Focal or task lighting is directive; it creates a bright spot that draws our attention, tells us what to look at, or orients us toward an important element or activity center in a space.

Foot-candle is a unit for measuring illumination that refers to the amount of light falling on a surface 1 foot (.3 meter) from a candle. General illumination should be from seven to ten foot-candles, while task lighting, depending on the task, can range from fifteen to 200 foot-candles.

Fluorescent lamps are a type of discharge lamp, which means that light is produced by the passage of an electric current through a vapor or gas instead of a tungsten wire, as in incandescent lamps. In this case, a fluorescent phosphor coating on the inside of the bulb transforms the electric energy into light.

General illumination is also called background or ambient lighting, and is the foundation of a lighting plan.

Halogen lamps are incandescent lamps, filled with halogen gas, that employ a tungsten filament. These lamps burn brighter and get much hotter than standard incandescent lamps.

Incandescent lamps are electric lamps in which a tungsten filament is heated by an electric current until it glows. This type of bulb is the most commonly found in homes.

Lamp is the correct term for what is commonly called a light bulb. It refers to the glass that encases a filament or holds some type of gas that glows when electricity is applied.

Lumens is an international unit that refers to the amount of light that a bulb produces.

Task lighting is also called focal lighting. It is bright, directed light that provides illumination adequate to accomplishing specific activities, such as reading, writing, playing games or working on crafts.

Torchiere is a floor lamp that directs light up to the ceiling rather than down, so it reflects off the ceiling to create a dramatic source of illumination.

Wattage is the amount of electrical current consumed by a bulb. A kilowatt is 1,000 watts.

>Photo Credits

>About the Authors

Lisa Skolnik is a regular contributor to the *Chicago Tribune* on design, entertaining, style and family issues, and also writes two nationally syndicated columns for the paper. Her work has also appeared in such publications as *Metropolitan Home* magazine, *Interiors* magazine, *Woman's Day*, *Good Housekeeping*, *Fodors* Chicago guidebook and more, and she is the author of 12 books on design. She lives and works in Chicago, where she is also the city editor for *Metropolitan Home*.

Nora Richter Greer is a freelance author/editor who has written about architecture and design for more than 20 years. She began her career at *Architecture* magazine. She is the author of and/or contributor to more than a dozen books, including *Architecture Transformed* (Rockport 1998), *Architecture as Response* (Rockport 1998), *The Search for Shelter* (AIA Press, 1995), and the forthcoming *Hot Dirt*, *Cool Straw* (Hearst Publications (2001). She resides in Washington, D.C.

Livia McRee is a craft designer and author. Born in Nashville and raised in New York City by her working artist parents, Livia has always been within a creative sphere. Her interests in writing led her toward an editorial position at *Handcraft Illustrated* magazine, which soon turned crafty. The magazine's focus on home decorating, sewing, and other arts prepared Livia for her career in craft design and publishing. More of Livia's how-to craft projects can be seen in *The Crafter's Project Book*. You can find out more about Livia at www.liviamcree.com.